SURVIVING THE EARLY LOSS OF A MOTHER

In memory of my mother and father, Susan and Frank Corey, and the mothers they lost so early in life, Ellen Higgins and Margaret Corey.

SURVIVING THE EARLY LOSS OF A MOTHER

Daughters Speak

Dr Anne Tracey

VERITAS

First published 2008 by
Veritas Publications
7/8 Lower Abbey Street
Dublin 1
Ireland
Email publications@veritas.ie
Website www.veritas.ie

ISBN 978 184730 130 7

Image © Getty Images, from the Hulton Archive, taken by Thurston Hopkins
Cover design by Lir Mac Cárthaigh
Printed in the Republic of Ireland by Colourbooks Ltd, Dublin

Veritas books are printed on paper made from the wood pulp of managed forests. For every
tree felled, at least one tree is planted, thereby renewing natural resources.

CONTENTS

Foreword	7
Introduction – The Beginning ...	9
1. The 'Silent Game'	23
2. 'Your Worst Nightmare'	43
3. 'Digging for Information'	69
4. 'Milestones in your Life'	87
5. 'You Learn to Cover Your Heart'	99
6. 'He was a Very Good Father'	132
Conclusion – The 'Incalculable' Loss	139
Suggested Reading	156
Acknowledgements	157

FOREWORD

This is a significant book that documents the real life experiences of women who lost their mothers as children. Since Anne Tracey has gathered the material for her research with great sensitivity, the testimonies provide authentic accounts of the lifelong impact of such a profound loss. The narratives are unfailingly moving, often through the fine detail of recollected experiences as seen through the eyes of the child at the time. We observe the dying mother's anguish about what will happen to the children; we almost see the little child craning from behind the mass of mourners to get a glimpse of the coffin as it is lowered into the ground; we witness the adult's reawakened grief as years later she discovers some fragment of information about how her mother died, or about what her mother was like. Too often, in a misguided attempt to 'protect' the child, the families surrounded the death with silence, so preventing the children from expressing their grief or, in some cases, from even understanding fully what had happened.

The women tell us of their enduring pain and of the deep longing for the mother that continues throughout the course of their lives. Each story is unique but certain patterns emerge. A central theme concerns the need for adults in the family and the community to reach out in a sensitive, understanding way to the grieving child and to continue to be aware of the child's complex array of emotions over time. Rituals and ceremonies should be adapted to take account of the child's grief. The dead mother's memory needs to be preserved, whether through boxes of letters, jewellery and photographs, or through family narratives, poems, songs or drawings. There needs to be a solemn farewell in whatever form is right for that particular child. There needs to be guidance for the adults involved, some of whom will also feel bereft, to offer the support the child needs. Most importantly, children need to know that it is safe to talk about the dead mother with someone they can trust.

Finally, this book documents the courage of the women who told their stories. They showed that, despite their tragic loss, they were able to build good lives in their families, through their professional work and in their communities. These brave women show us that life continues despite irreplaceable loss. I hope that this book brings hope to those who are going through such an experience.

Helen Cowie
Professor of Mental Health and Youth,
University of Surrey
September 2008

INTRODUCTION
THE BEGINNING ...

Dear Reader,

For one reason or another you have picked up this book that sets out to honour the loss of a mother in early life. It may be that you are a survivor of early loss and this is the first time you have come across a book that directly addresses your experience. It may be that your grandmother died when your mother was young and you want to gain more insight and understanding of her experience by reading other daughters' stories. Some of you may be interested in learning more about early loss and its impact. Whatever your reason for picking up this book, I hope it brings you whatever you need – insight and understanding, solace and comfort, reassurance, recognition, and maybe inspiration!

LOSS IS LOSS

It is nearly impossible to convey how loss of any kind, at any age, can severely disrupt an individual's internal state and external world. In whatever form it comes, loss takes its toll mentally, emotionally and physically. For example, the pain of the grief that is experienced through a miscarriage or stillbirth is unimaginable. Many of those who were parted with their baby at birth live with regret every day. A change in our health or the end of an important relationship brings devastation. When information is disclosed that alters a person's perceptions of themselves – as in the case, for example, of the adopted who remain for a time unaware of their circumstances – it turns their world upside down and leads to inner turmoil. When a parent is 'unreachable' due to alcohol or drugs, the consequences are far-reaching. For some, the loss of a beloved pet, the challenge of relocating to a new environment, or the loss of a job can be deeply upsetting at any stage in life. When faced with any life-altering, life-changing event, we can plummet into a spiral of grief that can seem never-ending, because, without question, loss changes us and changes our futures forever.

Even though there is almost daily evidence that life is not permanent and that the unexpected can and does happen, people hope that a natural order will prevail in their own lives and the lives of their families. Parents expect that their children will outlive them and children expect that their parents will live until they are, at least, in adulthood. It's something that we try not to think about because coming to terms with our own mortality and that of those we care about is not always easily achieved. When death and loss occurs, it serves as a reminder that we are not invincible, that, indeed, we are vulnerable human beings who are subject to the cycle of life and death.

The death of a loved one is a profoundly difficult, life-changing experience that everyone will encounter at some point in their lives. When we are bereaved, we grieve the loss of the person, the loss of what we had with them and the loss of the future that could have been. Perhaps many of you starting to read this book have come to know death, loss and grief intimately over your lifetime, as I feel I have.

MY PERSONAL STORY

I don't remember exactly when my six brothers, Frank, Jack, Brendan, Brian, Desmond and Michael, and I learned that we didn't have a grandmother on either side of the family. As in many families, the histories and legacies inherited by our elders gradually emerged as we grew up. I heard other children in primary school talking about their grannies and I began to realise that our situation was different. My mother lost her mother when she was six years old and my father's mother, Margaret, died when he was fourteen. The only living grandparent that I knew was my mother's dad, John Higgins, who lived until he was ninety-three!

During our growing-up years, Aunt Annie (my father's sister) became a kind of surrogate granny to us all and, for me, another role model. Annie was hardworking and highly motivated, she was stylish and cared about her appearance. She was one of the kindest people I have ever known. Throughout her life, Annie was used to the caring role. She was eight years older than my father when their mother died and consequently took over as 'mother' to her siblings and looked after their father, Patrick, until he died. Annie remained single all of her life and as time went on my brothers and I were part of her 'adopted' family. When I arrived at the latter end of six sons, she claimed me as her 'wee girl'. I was her long-awaited constant companion and became very attached to her as the years went on; we all did.

But the attentions of Annie did not detract me (or my brothers) from an acute awareness of the loss that my mother carried with her throughout her life. The death of her mother had left a visible, indelible mark; it was a legacy from which she never really recovered throughout her ninety years of life. Little did I know that the death of her mother, Ellen Higgins, in childbirth at the age of twenty-nine, would shape and profoundly influence my life in the years to come.

Like many children, I was inquisitive and wanted to hear about my maternal grandmother and what had happened to her. I was equally interested in learning about my father's mother and the circumstances of her untimely death. But my parents were (mostly) reluctant to talk; it upset them too much. As my brothers and I observed it, our mother and father both exhibited a deeply sensitive response to death and loss when it occurred in the family network, in the community where we lived or when it was reported on the news on the radio. It was a striking feature of their lives that was unmistakably present; death and loss struck a chord at a very deep level.

In listening to my mother's story of loss, I discovered that her own mother's death was imprinted on her mind. On the few occasions in her life when she did open up, she was particularly dejected and sad as she conveyed the details. It seemed that her family had tried to protect the children by allowing little contact and keeping them away from their very ill mother. But, being curious, my mother spoke about how she made her way unannounced into the living room of her home, from where she could see into her mother's bedroom. She recalled that there was a 'bath of blood' and overheard her mother saying to her father, 'What will the children do now, John?'

This was a stressful and traumatic, life-changing experience for a six year old to take in and deal with, especially when no-one talked about the death and the loss. It seemed that there was little help available to work through the trauma and the tragedy of the untimely death. A remarkable feature of life then was the inability of anyone to help or support the bereaved children in the grief that they all undoubtedly felt at the time and in the years following. My mother resignedly concluded that, in that era, death was rarely spoken about with children.

Ellen Higgins was central in her children's lives. Reportedly, she was a kind mother and a beautiful lady who treasured her offspring. The loss of her changed the lives of the entire family forever. In the aftermath, my grandfather, John, my mother, Susan, her two sisters and brother went to live with their paternal grandmother. Ellen, wife and mother, was deeply missed by everyone.

Over the years, I reflected on my mother's experience, not only on the loss she suffered but the repercussions. I was aware of the fact that losing her mother and the hard life that followed had taken its toll on her. My father too had endured the early loss of his mother and undoubtedly suffered as a consequence. He was a hardworking man who took his responsibilities in life very seriously. While he was anxious in his own way, he was a social being. I often thought he was saved from despair partly through his love of company and craic and his ability to entertain a roomful of people with stories and songs. He had a unique style and amazed and entertained us all with songs that he learned as a young boy. Some had umpteen verses, but rarely did he forget a word or a line.

In contrast, my mother's way of being was distinctly different. While she was devoted and worked tirelessly to meet the needs of her family – cooking, cleaning, knitting, baking – at times she seemed locked away in a world that was inaccessible to those around her. She was not a conversationalist, and indeed rarely talked at length about anything, choosing instead to quietly observe and listen. However, she was most vocal when it came to our homework or schooling – in this respect she was always willing to contribute. She was an intelligent woman who had lost out on her own much desired education. The loss of opportunity made her fiercely interested in promoting our learning and development. She was always encouraging us to learn and always ready to help with school work, but, be assured, she had her work cut out for her with us all! During one phase in second-level education I found it very difficult to concentrate and my mind wouldn't settle on things. Later I realised that perhaps it was a knock-on effect of life as I knew it at the time.

When I was around fifteen years old my mother had to spend time away from us to get well. Her life history weighed heavily on her, and as the years went on her physical, mental and emotional health collapsed. She became clinically depressed. It was particularly difficult when we visited her. We felt deeply sad seeing her and leaving her. She looked lost, distant, remote, and it was hard to 'connect' with her. Eventually, she returned home and lived well for many years with the help of medication and a loving family around her. At the time, however, her treatment did not include therapy or counselling, and I often wondered if, at some point, she had had the opportunity to talk to someone about her life experiences, might the breakdown in her health have been avoided.

It wasn't until I returned to study as a mature student that I began to reflect much more on my mother, father and Annie and what they had to endure in their lives. The learning gained through studies in psychology had brought insights and personal enlightenment that helped me to know and understand the family, myself and the human psyche somewhat better than I had previously. However, tragedy struck! Just as I was nearing the end of the first year of a four-year course, the doctor who was treating my father in hospital informed me in March 1989 that my father's time was limited; he had possibly three to four months to live. I felt as if someone had kicked me in the stomach and taken the breath out of my body. I was thrown into a state of disbelief and despair. He died on 26 July of that year and the loss of him was shattering for all of us. I missed him desperately because we had a tremendous father–daughter bond.

It's no surprise that my interest in how people experience loss through death deepened as the years went on. Through personal experience I had learned about loss and grief, and over the years the history of loss embedded in the lives of my parents and over the years family circle had seeped into my psyche. In particular, as a daughter I witnessed close at hand my mother dealing with the psychological ramifications of the loss of her mother and the loss of her third son, who was still-born. The later bereavement compounded the earlier loss of her mother; it re-triggered deep feelings of sadness and grief.

BEREAVEMENT CARE

The desire to get into the area of helping the bereaved as soon as I graduated felt right to me. I welcomed the opportunity to train as a volunteer with Cruse Bereavement Care, Foyle Branch in Derry city, Northern Ireland. Counselling bereaved and people supervising practitioners in their work over many years taught me that the journey through loss and grief is, indeed, a unique and personal experience, and yet that the bereaved share common psychological reactions in their response to loss, such as sadness, anger, depression and, for some over time, acceptance and adjustment.

Working with the bereaved also revealed that while adults may seek counselling in the aftermath of a recent bereavement, other losses, including early loss experiences, could emerge in the therapeutic process. A client may carry repressed and unresolved grief from childhood into their adult lives. At the time of the death there may have been little opportunity to express or share feelings of grief, and as time elapsed there may have been a sense of 'it's too late to talk' or perhaps of not knowing who to talk to. In bereavement literature, bereaved children are sometimes referred to as the 'forgotten mourners', as their need to address their feelings of grief is often overlooked by adult members of the family (who are often trying to protect the young by sheltering them from the pain of the loss).

Working in the field of bereavement counselling had shown me that the opportunity to share their stories can help many bereaved people to work through and resolve their feelings of loss and grief. Gaining a voice in a confidential setting can be part of the healing process for many. The combination of being personally bereaved and later working as a practitioner convinced me that the more we know about the meaning of a loss and the course of grief that follows, the better equipped we will be to provide the help and support that bereaved people need.

In the course of the intervening years I reached a landmark in my life: I became a mother. Having my own children made me begin to *really* appreciate and understand the commitment and dedication that our parents had shown to us down the years. However, it wasn't until I was *in* the mother role that I began to get a measure of how well prepared I was for it. It was then I began to realise that motherhood requires a well-nourished set of internal resources. At times, I reflected on my mother's experience and what it must have been like for her when she became a mother. If I was feeling somewhat depleted at times, how must she have felt? It was during the five years I spent in psychotherapy (which coincided with my doctoral research) that I started to realise and appreciate the extent to which my mother's experience of loss and the repercussions it imposed on her had shaped her as a person and, in turn, had a hand in shaping me too.

I came to the point where I had to make a decision about the topic of my doctoral studies. After working independently for some years following graduation, I had secured a post at the University of Ulster as a lecturer and it was imperative that I got started on my PhD. Dr Mary Gallagher, a colleague, role model and one of the supervisors of my study, patiently helped me to examine and explore possible areas of research. I was drawn to the idea of a study in the area of counselling or bereavement, or perhaps one that incorporated both. Any attempts to collate my thoughts in writing were carefully read and reviewed by Dr Gallagher. It was a process that took time, but one that will be forever appreciated because it allowed me to come to a firm conclusion about my study. In the end, my choice was synonymous with the learning that I had achieved through studies in psychology, bereavement work and personal experience – I wanted to explore the experiences of daughters bereaved of their mothers in early life.

In preparation for my study, I began to delve into the research in bereavement, loss and grief. The existing research showed that the early loss of a mother can lead to emotional, behavioural and mental health problems for survivors in the short-term and long-term. While there was a vast amount of literature available, I was drawn to the fact that little had been written in Ireland about the early loss of a mother. (Rather than try to elaborate on the research here, I thought it might be useful to include a list of reading material at the end of the book for those of you who might be interested in further reading.) I was aware that only a few studies had concentrated solely on the experiences of daughters bereaved of a mother in childhood, or examined the impact of maternal loss over the lifespan. Therefore, it seemed that more needed to be known about the meaning of the loss and how it impacted or affected daughters' lives at the time and in the intervening years. What had been helpful or unhelpful in their journey through loss and grief could also be explored. Equally, it would be useful to find out what had made a significant difference to survivors in their journey, or what factors might improve the quality of life for the early bereaved.

I hoped that my research would help to raise the profile and increase awareness of early bereavement in Ireland – put the early bereaved on the map, so to speak. Equally, giving a 'voice' to adult daughters might help to provide insights for those in the population with a personal history of maternal loss in childhood, those who will face a similar loss in the future, and for anyone interested in knowing more about the impact of early loss of a mother. In addition, knowing more about the experience and meaning of the early loss of a mother could help to inform and enlighten those in the medical or therapeutic professions who help and support the bereaved. The study could also be an opportunity to alert families, communities and society at large to the needs of daughters bereaved of a mother in early life.

I decided that the most appropriate way to begin the process of investigating the phenomenon of the early loss of a mother with daughters in Ireland was to invite survivors in the general population to be interviewed. And so began the study that is the foundation of this book. It was an incredible journey of learning and enlightenment, and I feel privileged to have had the opportunity to facilitate the exploration of experiences of early loss with the women who courageously agreed to be interviewed.

THE STUDY

The aim of the study was to gain insight into the phenomenon of early maternal loss from the perspective of adult daughters. Twenty-six women who were maternally bereaved between birth and eleven years were selected to enlighten us on the meaning of early loss and its impact across the lifespan.

The opportunity to share their experiences was welcomed by all those who were interviewed, as reflected in Louise's comment that bereaved daughters are 'not left out in the wilderness anymore'. However, when they rang to inquire about the research, a few daughters suggested that their families would not be pleased if they knew that they were thinking about taking part in the study. One respondent suggested that the family's attitude to talking about the loss of their mother, particularly after the number of years that had passed, would be, 'let sleeping dogs lie!' For this reason, perhaps, some declined to take part, even though they were assured of anonymity and confidentiality.

Six of the women who took part were reared in the Republic of Ireland, mainly County Donegal, and the remaining twenty were from various regions of Northern Ireland. Their ages ranged between twenty-five and seventy-seven; the average age was thirty-two. Thirteen of the women were married, five were single, three widowed, two divorced, two co-habiting, and one was separated. Careers where in the fields of teaching, nursing, homemaking, community groups, school meals, banking, administration and business. Some had returned to education.

To ensure that the study was ethically sound, none of the women who participated was known to me personally or had been a former client in my role as a counsellor. It was also important to exclude anyone who was in psychotherapy, counselling or undergoing psychiatric treatment. Due to the emotive nature of the research, it was felt that participating in the study might interfere with the therapeutic process, perhaps causing disturbance or anxiety to those currently receiving help. However, each of those interviewed was offered a list of support agencies to assure them that help was available should they require it following the interview.

The deaths of the participants' mothers occurred between the 1930s and the 1980s, with the highest number of deaths – twelve – occurring in the 1970s. The mothers' ages at death ranged between twenty-nine and forty-nine, sixteen of whom died in their thirties, eight in their forties and two in their late twenties. The causes of death included cancer, childbirth, accident, septacemia, thrombosis, brain haemorrage, heart disease, miscarriage, emphysema and death through violence. The most frequently reported cause of death was cancer, which occurred in nine cases.

Following the interviews and the rigorous, systematic analysis that interview material requires, all daughters were sent a summary of the findings. They were invited to provide written feedback and/or attend a focus group session to verify that the 'story' of the research was accurate.

Five participants were able to attend the focus group session. The following questions were posed to help verify the outcome of the study:

* Do you recognise yourself in the summary?
* Are the parts of the summary that you can relate to adequately explained? If not, perhaps you could suggest what might be included to make it a better explanation.
* Are there important aspects of early maternal loss and its impact that have not been included in the study so far?

In addition to the feedback provided by the daughters in the study, verification of the interviews was sought through two professionals, Carole and Nicola, who worked in the field of bereavement care. The review of two randomly selected interview transcripts was an important part of the research process. It helped me gain other perspectives and alternative views about the content of the interviews. The raters were asked to read and analyse the interview as they saw it and make notes about their interpretations. It was a very productive process and very much appreciated. Both transcripts were returned within one month and some very useful comments offered.

While the deaths of mothers had occurred when daughters were aged between birth and eleven, their experiences – shared with honesty and courage in the interviews – were unique to each individual, and yet contained common features in relation to reactions, coping and not coping. The salient themes that emerged through the testimonies are addressed in the individual chapters of this book, namely, The Silent Game, Your Worst Nightmare, Digging for Information, Milestones in Your Life, You Learn to Cover Your Heart, He was a Very Good Father and The Incalculable Loss. These chapter titles are phrases from the testimonies of the various daughters.

As you will see in the chapters ahead, the significant and important influences that underpinned daughters' experiences of early childhood bereavement were the life-long impact of the death and loss of their mother *and* the multitude of ramifications that unfolded. Central to both strands was the role of surviving adults, their response to the illness and death, the management of the bereavement (before, during and after the loss) within families and the circumstances within which daughters were reared.

The purpose of writing this book was to ensure that daughters' voices are 'heard', that the loss of a mother in early life is validated, acknowledged and recognised, and that perhaps those with a personal history of early loss might find solace and comfort in the experiences of others. Equally, the testimonies of daughters might give others the courage to speak of their own loss.

OTHER BEREAVED GROUPS DESERVE ATTENTION

Since I began disseminating the study at conferences (in Ireland and England) in the past number of years, the response from delegates has been tremendous. Those in attendance, many of them early loss survivors, wholeheartedly agreed that the study was necessary. However, while the study and now the book have concentrated solely on daughters bereaved of their mothers, it is important for me to say that I was not ignoring the fact that other groups of bereaved people in this country deserve to be studied and need attention.

At a recent counselling psychology conference in Trinity College, Dublin, where I was presenting my study, at least half a dozen males were present in the audience of around fifty or so. The question about research with early-bereaved sons was raised. In response, I indicated that, indeed, I appreciated and was aware that early loss in males in Ireland needs to be explored and written about. However, I explained that I had made a personal choice to concentrate on daughters and undertake a study that I felt was manageable within a specified time frame.

In the course of more informal discussions with practising psychologists, further areas of need became evident. For example, one practitioner who was then working with daughters of alcoholic mothers in Ireland said that they too suffer the same psychological effects as the early-bereaved. However, she qualified this by saying that perhaps the 'bereaved' through alcohol group have more enduring anger because their mother is present but inaccessible. Another area of concern was that of daughters who have been separated from their mothers in life; they too require attention. I welcomed these discussions and agreed wholeheartedly that there is much that remains unknown about different 'bereaved' groups in Ireland that could be explored through research with survivors.

As you will see in the course of reading this book, the daughters show that they were, indeed, resourceful! They have found ingenious and innovative ways of coping and taking care of themselves. Along the way they developed a resilience through their own efforts and through recognition of any source of support that was available. In essence, they showed themselves to be strong and courageous survivors of early loss.

My hope is that this book will help to bring an end to silence, exclusion and misunderstanding, and mark the beginning of a new era of awareness, recognition, understanding, acknowledgement and validation.

I trust that you will find it helpful.
Anne
September 2008

1. THE 'SILENT GAME'

It was very much like a silent game, and that was my father's way of dealing with it. His way of thinking was, don't upset them – Patricia.

When a mother's life reaches an untimely end, the family descend into a state of shock, numbness and disbelief. While people may search for something to say, meaningful words are hard to find. As adults struggle to make sense of the loss, the enormity of what has happened cannot be expressed out loud. The temptation is to think that children can be protected or sheltered from the stark reality of the death by being kept away from the rituals of the wake or funeral, or by being given little information about the details of what has happened. The effort to keep things as normal as possible and to avoid discussion of the painful truth for the children's sake can be the well-intentioned aim of adults in the hours, days, months and even years ahead. But young children are perceptive; they are aware of being 'shut out from everything' in the midst of the turmoil around them.

As daughters who have suffered the early loss of their mother will confirm, life is never the same again. It is divided into two halves – the life before a mother's death and the time when she is no longer there. And the two worlds are very different places. The home is not the place it once was, the family has lost its central figure and the future seems bleak and uncertain. Whether you are an infant of a few weeks old, a few months old, a few years old; whether you are already walking and talking, or you are four or five and have started school; whether you are six, seven, eight, nine, ten or eleven years of age at the time, the death of your mother is a devastating blow. The life you knew comes to an end, sometimes with little warning. In the aftermath, the struggle to survive begins.

The death of a mother can be a sudden event that imposes an instant or immediate change on the family. In some cases, a mother's death can be the result of an accident, violence, childbirth or a miscarriage. It can also be caused by a brain haemorrhage, septicaemia, emphysema or thrombosis. Sometimes, the change that comes about in family life starts to develop when a mother becomes ill with cancer or heart problems. In their concerted efforts to protect the children and their sick mother, adults monitor events closely but say little to the young about what is going on. However, the absence of information can only add to the burden of a child's loss.

'WE DIDN'T REALLY REALISE WHAT WAS WRONG WITH MAMMY'

When her mother was ill with cancer, Kathleen had no idea of what was to come:

I didn't know she was going to die. I just thought that Mammy's sick. There was no talk of her having a severe illness, having a serious illness. There was no mention of it at all.

Lesley recalls visiting the hospital but reflects that she was sheltered from it all:

I was six and my brother was three. We didn't really understand at that time what the illness was, or even what a hospital was.

At the time, very little was explained to Elaine:

I guess I sort of knew that she'd had an operation, but I can't think of anybody sitting down and saying, 'your mum's been ill'.

Elizabeth, whose mother died at the age of forty-one, when she was ten, suggests that she and her sisters were naive:

We didn't really realise what was wrong with Mammy. We always thought that she had been going into the hospital with her teeth.

When a mother is not well, children become acutely sensitive to things that are happening around them. The behaviour of adults and anything unusual does not escape them: an aunt waits at the school gate instead of the mother; grandparents, 'whom you don't expect to be crying', are visibly upset; there is a commotion at home. The doctor's daily visits are silently observed and pondered over, but not discussed. Pauline poignantly recalls a scene from the time her mother was ill in bed with cancer:

> The doctor used to meet us at the turn of the stairs everyday. He must have been up to give her an injection because we heard her crying before he came and we heard nothing after.

At the time, the details of such events can remain unexplained and unquestioned. As Theresa states plainly:

> I didn't know that she was going to die.

In the middle of it all, the child can become an onlooker, an observer who is given few explanations. If children have questions, they may have difficulty in knowing who to ask. Daughters would have liked to talk to their mother but because of her illness they were kept away from her.

'WE WEREN'T ALLOWED TO GO IN'

Dara remembers being determined to see her mother and found ways to slip into her bedroom:

> I went into my mammy's room and her partner said 'Don't be going into your mammy, she's not well', but I sneaked in.

Pauline recalls how time with her mother was forbidden:

> We weren't allowed to go in, you know. We wouldn't have seen her for weeks at a time. She was only next door in the bedroom.

Some daughters found that if they did succeed in getting in to see their mother, they were asked to leave in a very short space of time, as Kathleen recollects:

She was in bed for weeks and weeks and weeks and I just remember going up to the bedroom occasionally and sitting with her for a while. But then people were coming in telling me to leave the room, 'Out you go', 'Come on, out you go'.

What these women later realised is that, at the time of their mother's illness, they were unknowingly moving towards an event that was to influence the rest of their lives. Yet, they did not get to spend time with their mother. The silence was maintained and it left them ill-prepared for what was to come.

THE LAST PICTURE

Helen had little idea of what was to unfold when she witnessed her mother leaving for the hospital:

The last picture I have of her is walking out of the house, down the path, into an ambulance, but I didn't know what it was about.

Helen explains that she didn't know her mother was going in to have a baby. Before the day was out her mother had died in childbirth. She explains:

At nine years of age, believe it or not, I didn't know what pregnancy was. I didn't know how babies were born, so therefore I didn't know that my mammy had gone into hospital to have a baby. You just weren't told anything. So I remember things getting increasingly tense as the day went on, and she died between 5.15 p.m. and 5.30 p.m. that evening.

Helen adds:

It was the fact that I was shut out from everything that had an impact on me, a lasting impact. I think those sorts of things will live with me forever.

Abbey, whose mother died as the result of an accidental fall, attempted to wake her mother on the morning following the ill-fated event:

I remember going into her bedroom to wake her up and found it very strange because she wouldn't wake up. I learned later on that she was in a coma at this stage. I went to my older sister and said, 'I can't wake up Mummy', and she was old enough to realise that something was wrong and called an ambulance, and that was the last I saw of her. I remember my dad calling myself and my sister to say that she wasn't coming home and that was it.

Dara too found her mother in a coma, when she went to seek permission to go to a friend's confirmation:

I went into my mammy's room to ask her could I go to the confirmation and I couldn't get her to wake up. It was the same day she went into hospital.

Within a few hours of putting her young children to bed with words of reassurance and comfort, Patricia's mother was shot dead in the backyard of her home by a British army soldier. Literally overnight, she was gone. Patricia describes the scene:

My mother used to knit; she sat in the chair and, as all youngsters do, we would sit at our mammy's feet. I had Mammy going to bed that night, putting us up to bed and saying, 'I'll see you in the morning', and then we came down to nothing. I mean to absolute nothing. She wasn't there and that was it; she was gone and the void just starts from that.

The loss took its toll on the family, particularly Patricia's father:

My father never spoke about it; half of him died that night as well. I mean, he never ever actually got over it.

At the age of nine, Alison was a back-seat passenger in the fatal car crash that ended her mother's life. But she didn't realise at the time that her mother was killed instantly in the front seat of the car:

I can still remember, and it's twenty-nine years ago, my mother slumped in the front of the car. My brothers and I were taken in an ambulance, and at this stage we didn't know what had happened – we were so young. I was left in a cubicle on my own. I didn't know where my father was, my brothers, or where my mum was.

THE FINAL WORDS

What many do not realise is that a mother's parting message has a profound and deep psychological effect on a child. When there is an echo of her promise to 'see you' at a later time, a child really believes that she will walk in through the door again. If a mother makes a promise, the young mind is convinced that she will keep that promise. It can take a long time to accept that that it is not going to happen. According to Anne, her mother was 'a very strong character' who was very much in her life. She explains what happened on the day her mother was killed in a road accident a short time after leaving the house:

> The morning she left, she woke me to say goodbye. Unfortunately she said, 'I'll see you on Tuesday, please God', and that will always stay in my head. Suddenly not to have her – for a long time I went through this thing thinking she was testing to see if I really loved her and she was going to walk back in the door, because there was no closure really.

Jennifer tearfully relives the last moments she had with her mother:

> Seeing the ambulance coming up the lane and not being able to believe that an ambulance was coming for my mother. She was sitting in the chair and the ambulance men were coming in and I remember crying and she said, 'Don't you cry, because if you cry, I'll cry', and that was the last time I ever saw her.

HEARING THE NEWS OF THE DEATH

There is no easy way to tell a child that their mother is dead and that they won't be seeing her again. Adults grappling with their own grief and perhaps in fear of having to deal with a child's sorrow can make a brief and sober statement: 'God took your mammy to heaven'; 'Well, that's your mummy away today'; 'She's gone'. The words sound stark and final. Deep down the child may get a sense that questions are not invited or welcome. However, the worst feeling of all is being 'left in the dark'.

Sometimes the news of the death is postponed for as long as possible. Anne knew that something was wrong and was desperate to know the truth. In the end it was 'nearly a relief' when she was finally told. Dara remembers the news being divulged on the way to her mother's funeral:

> I was told on the way to her requiem Mass that she had died. I thought I was just going to Mass.

When her father told Elizabeth that her mother had died she couldn't take it in:

> Daddy had come in and told me that Mammy had died and I wouldn't even get out of bed. I kept thinking, is she, or has he just told me that. I can remember just feeling numb.

On hearing that 'God wanted your mammy in heaven', Jennifer became hysterical. She didn't really understand what exactly this meant but she knew that it was final. The explanation given to Lesley, who was six at the time, was similar. A relative took on the task of telling her the news, and that there would be no more visits to the hospital:

> She sat me on her knee and she said, 'You can't visit your mother anymore'. I said, 'Okay' and she said, 'Do you understand why', and I said 'No'. She said, 'She has died and gone to heaven to be with the angels' and I said, 'Right, okay'. And she said, 'Right, okay'. And I went and I played. That was how I found out.

Like many other children, Alison and her siblings cried when they were told of their mother's death following the road accident that put the entire family in hospital. The nurse's response has stuck with Alison for twenty-nine years:

> 'What are you crying for? There's no need to cry.'

The resentment she felt at being chastised for crying about the loss of her mother remains with her today.

THE WAKE

Whether or not children are included in the mourning rituals depends upon the family's attitude to how such things should be managed, to the era, to the children's age and level of understanding and to the circumstances at home.

Often, the lack of clear communication or silence that has prevailed throughout the illness and death continues through the wake and funeral. Even when daughters are permitted to take part in the mourning rituals in some way, many report it is rare to be offered the emotional help and support that they needed. So there is little outlet for their feelings.

Adults may not realise that following the death of a mother, young children can harbour disturbing thoughts. Not having had the opportunity to see her can lead to years of worry, Anne reveals:

> *The only time I saw her coffin was when I was in the church, and actually, years and years later, I used to have nightmares about what she must have looked like; because it was a car crash, you assume the worst.*

It wasn't until she was in her late teens that Anne found out that there was only a 'little bruise' on her mother's cheek.

There are unexpected situations that can arise in the lives of bereaved children that they may not share within the family. For example, during the wake, children may be 'sent away' to relatives in an attempt to shield them from death and sorrow. But Helen E found it tremendously hard to accept that her friends on the street had seen her mother and she hadn't:

> *My friends were able to talk about seeing my mammy in the coffin and I didn't see her. You know how children are curious, and they went into the wake house and they saw my mammy. At the time I found that hard to deal with.*

Being allowed to see their deceased mother in the coffin can help to give closure to children. Elizabeth says:

> *We never saw her in the coffin, so I always thought that maybe she*

wasn't actually dead. With the coffin being closed, I was lying in bed thinking, sure maybe she could come in through the door tomorrow. I know she is supposed to be dead, but you didn't actually see her dead. That's the one thing I regret not seeing.

However, if the choice is made to allow children to see their deceased mother, the way in which this is managed should be given careful consideration. Pauline explained that she and her sister were 'pushed' into the room where her mother was being waked, but were unsure what to do because they didn't know what they were going to see. Pauline immediately realised that it was her mother and that she wasn't alive; because it had been so long since she'd seen her Pauline had to touch her to make sure it was true! Her prevailing memory was that her mother was laid out in pink, a colour that she has detested for many years.

For some, like Maude, seeing her mother was something she cherished in later years. She recalls with a sense of gladness her memory of the time, still fresh in her mind after seventy years. Her older sisters invited her to go in and see her mother in the coffin. At first she was unsure if she wanted to go in; however, looking back she is glad that she did:

I was hesitant. I said, 'I don't know if I want to go in'. But I braved it and I thought she was lovely. And I said, 'Look at the lovely gown she has on', you know the way she was all in white. The coffin was all white and I can see her to this day in it.

As Maude discovered, the support and understanding of the family can help children to overcome uncertainty about seeing their mother, enabling them to retain a positive memory and positive image of her.

THE FUNERAL

A mother's funeral is a time when sensitivity to the needs and wishes of the children is called for. What is going on inside of the child is mostly hidden from view, as Kathleen, whose mother died in the 1970s, summarises:

> *It was very difficult at that time because people didn't realise that children grieved as much as adults do. In fact it's worse, because they don't understand what's happening around them.*

When you are young, you have to conform to the wishes of adults, especially concerning matters of whether or not you will attend your mother's funeral service. In past years, the protocol was that 'ladies didn't go to funerals', so in order to be taken you had to 'kick up a fuss', as Alison did. Having fought to get to the funeral, she found it frustrating to be kept back from the graveside while the rest of the family were beside it:

> *My older brother and my younger brother were there beside Daddy at the graveside, and I was standing at the back of this crowd of men. I thought, why am I standing here, I want to be there with my father.*

She was nine at the time. On the day of her mother's funeral, it took spiritedness on Anne's part to make sure that she was part of the family group in the church:

> *My father and my two sisters were up in the front and eventually I moved my way up. I wasn't one to sit back.*

There is, however, a sense that fathers want to protect the young due to fears about the impact that the funeral might have on them. Elaine recollects her dad's views on the matter:

> *He didn't want us to see her being put into the ground, he thought it might have a bad effect.*

However, being 'kept away' can lead to regrets. As Abbey explains:

> *I remember my dad going to the funeral, but he thought that myself and my other sisters were not prepared for it, or he didn't want us to see anything, and that's the one thing I do actually regret.*

What is more difficult is that when the funeral is taboo, other rituals may also become taboo. The consequences of not attending the funeral are long-term, as Abbey went on to explain:

> None of us have ever been to her grave. I don't think any of us ever will now – it's been twenty-four years. None of us have ever been.

The day of her mother's funeral stands out 'very clearly' in Mary B's mind. She was seven at the time and wasn't attending the service. Mary B describes how she got up on the wall to get a view of the funeral procession as it left her home to make its way to where her ancestors were buried. She observes:

> I could see the whole funeral cortege, and it seemed to go very far.

Pauline too has vivid memories but recalls the day of her mother's funeral with feelings of frustration. As she remembers, she was 'dragged up the road' away from the funeral but was still able to see the procession in the distance. Theresa candidly reminds us that:

> People forget that children have thoughts and feelings. Just because you are young, it doesn't mean that you don't hurt or you don't feel anything.

'THINGS WERE NEVER EVER THE SAME AGAIN'

In the days following the death, everything takes on a new form and meaning. The routine of life is 'shattered', replaced by a sense of disorder and disarray. Without their mother, children are sensitive to every little change that takes place in daily living. The sense of security that was once present is eroded. It is not only the loss of routine that is deeply felt, it is the loss of a mother's touch, her way of doing things that is different to any other. Patricia, whose mother died when she was nine, conveys in heartfelt words how the normal, everyday things in life were deeply affected by the loss:

> Things were never ever the same again ... it was a completely different way of life – a completely different way of getting breakfast, of doing your homework, of getting your hair fixed. Even to put a bow in your hair was different because nobody did it the way she did it.

If a child is in infancy or very young at the time, they may not remember losing their mother, but they grow up in a world that is overshadowed by her death. Maggie, who was five months old when her mother died, explains that the death was always around, always part of her childhood for as long as she can remember. As life goes on, children sometimes learn 'second hand' about their mother's life, illness and death from those around them. Gradually, little nuggets of information help to give a glimpse of the time of her death and beyond. Maggie's older sister told her about the day their mother died:

> My sister remembers very clearly the day that she died. She remembers me being in a Moses basket, and then being taken away, and she said that was the last time she saw me.

Liz was five months old at the time and didn't find out until she was in her forties that her mother was carrying another child when she died and that her sudden death was caused by 'severe thrombosis'. She never had any doubt that her mother was dead because she had been told very, very early on. However, no-one had made a point of telling her what had happened; in later years 'it just cropped up in conversation'.

Other news brings a mixture of comfort and sadness. Louise thoughtfully reflects on the relationship that existed between herself and her mother:

> I was told that she did breastfeed me, she always had me with her. When she was lying in bed for a year with the cancer, it was me that she had in with her at the time. Literally the day before she died she still had me; they had to take me out of her arms.

When a young child is told out of the blue, 'That's not our mammy, our mammy's dead', it comes as a 'terrible blow', as it did to Elena, who hadn't realised that the aunt who had been caring for her since she was two weeks old wasn't her mother. She recalls the moment when the news was announced:

It was terrible. I just couldn't believe it. I just wondered what she was like. You saw other children with their mammies and you always knew that you hadn't got that.

'I WAS JUST KICKING, SCREAMING AND SHOUTING'

When your mother dies, when she is 'taken away', it is a total shock to the system. All sorts of strange and unfamiliar feelings erupt. There is confusion, abandonment, isolation and loneliness. When the young mind is overloaded in this way, it is difficult to cope and the extreme distress needs to be released somehow. Lesley lay on the floor kicking, screaming and shouting, at the age of six, in the days following her mother's death. Elaine's mother passed away when she was five and she recalls the pain she felt:

I was crying my heart out; I was crying for my mother.

At times like these, it is not easy to be comforted and reassured and, in the devastation, there may be few around who are able to offer support. The adults are also suffering and confused and, in the midst of their own pain and despair, they do not always know how to manage in the situation.

MULTIPLE LOSSES

Not only is the aftermath of a death a time of change and confusion, it can also be a time of major upheaval for the family, the ramifications of which are many. It is not only the end of the relationship with their mother that is difficult to deal with, but daughters also have to bear the brunt of the changes that come about as a result of her death. It is a time when 'unseen' losses escape the attention of others; they can go unacknowledged.

The loss takes its toll on relationships. Fathers grappling with their own loss are unable to talk about the death. As they become locked in their own grief, they are less emotionally or physically accessible to those around them, including their children. In some cases, relatives (especially those on the mother's side of the family) may fade out of the picture. As a result, important friendships or relationships with aunts, uncles and cousins may be lost and not redeemed for many years.

Adults may be concerned about how the children will be looked after and have to make tough decisions about the future. Plans are made in which the children have little say. For some families, this might mean relocating to a different home or even a different country. Others face a future where they are reared apart from their siblings, or, in some instances, all of the children move to be reared with family members, away from the adults they know. Relatives may feel it is their 'duty' to help, but some reluctantly take on the task of rearing a family of bereaved young children. Living in such circumstances can be a source of regret for bereaved children; they become sensitive to the 'messages' that are transmitted in the household. In a climate of 'no emotional love and feeling beholden', it is difficult to turn to adult carers for help and support.

Another dimension to the multiple losses that can occur in the aftermath of a mother's death is the trauma of losing the person who is or has become a loved and meaningful father figure. Being deprived of a father or the father figure they love profoundly affects the young, as Dara found. She regarded it as a 'double blow' when she had to leave the home she knew and the person she had come to regard as her father. For a young girl, this is an unwelcome change as it means the end of another important relationship in her life, one that she yearns for endlessly in the years ahead. Dara, who was ten when her mother died, speaks of her experience:

> I think the hardest thing of all, apart from her death, was that the only other person we were as close to was her partner; we lost him as well, so it was a double blow.

In the midst of the pain and sorrow and trying to decide what is best, the importance of the attachments that have been developed can be overlooked.

Some daughters may find that there is a reversal of roles, whereby caring for others unexpectedly becomes part of their responsibility in their 'new' life. Depending on circumstances, this can mean helping to look after the needs of younger siblings, or in some cases the needs of elderly relatives that the children have been assigned to live with. As time goes on, adjusting to a replacement mother figure is another challenge for bereaved children. It is not only the death and loss of a mother that a young daughter is grieving, she is grieving the life she knew.

NOBODY TO TALK TO

It didn't matter where they lived or whom they lived with after their mothers' death, daughters found that silence prevailed. In the aftermath, mothers became a 'closed subject', their names were rarely mentioned. Many reported facing a life journey with little understanding or clarity regarding what had happened and why. The approach adopted by families is reflected in Theresa's words:

Everybody got on with what they were doing and hoped for the best.

Everything becomes shrouded in secrecy and mystery and that is how things remained, indefinitely. Alison, aged thirty-eight, said it was only recently that she was able to approach an uncle to ask about her 'mum', and it was too long a wait, she said. Helen E maintains that being 'shut out from everything' had a lasting impact:

Things like not being at the wake or not being at the funeral; what had happened not being explained to me; the fear that we were all going to be separated – those things come back to me from time to time.

Even in the enduring silence, according to Mary, there was a desire to find out more:

> *The loss of my mammy was never mentioned afterwards. My father was one of these types of people – you don't ask questions, you don't ask 'those kind of things', and that was the end to asking questions. I would have loved to have been able to ask questions, you know, 'Where did you meet my mammy?' I would have loved to have gone down that road with him, but he was one of those men that was old-fashioned in their ways.*

Children learn that if the adults are 'physically or emotionally' unable to talk about the death, it becomes nearly impossible to ask questions. Teresa recalls:

> *We would never have brought her up with him anyway because he couldn't cope. He would have burst out crying at the kitchen table – he couldn't handle it.*

Jennifer explains that they tried not to talk about the death of her mother,

> *... because if you mentioned it, Daddy would start to cry. I can definitely remember hearing him cry during the night.*

To prevent the adults from being sad, questions were avoided, as Elizabeth confides:

> *I never wanted to upset anybody that was close to her so we didn't ask.*

HELPING CHILDREN TO COPE

More than anything, children need the support of a trusted adult to help them to cope with the loss and to understand all the strange feelings they are experiencing. The bereaved daughters wanted and needed someone (their father, another family member or a trusted adult) to explain things to them in a way that would have helped them to understand what had happened to their mother and why she died. Being sensitive to the needs of a bereaved child can make a difference, as Ann explains:

We were meant to start school that September but Daddy must have kept us off for a year. You were still very traumatised, kicking and screaming. We didn't want to be apart from Daddy; just obviously very upset.

When you lose your mother, your father or whoever else you are close to consequently become an extremely important part of your life. You need to be in close proximity to them; there is a fear that they might die too.

In shielding or protecting children from the truth, adults may have thought that they were saving them from being distressed. While it can be difficult to voice feelings about a death, and time alone is sometimes what the bereaved desire, there also comes a time when talking is welcomed. The consensus amongst the daughters is that talking would have helped.

Dara recognises that the adults thought they were protecting the children, but she is firm in her mind that talking would have made a difference in the long run:

It would have been so different and so much easier had they talked about her and had they encouraged us to talk about her. You know that whole talking through where you need to talk, that would have been a God-send. I'm sure they thought they were doing the right thing; maybe they didn't want to bring up her name in case we were upset. But why not let us be upset – is that not all part of the healing? Let us be upset.

However, not everyone feels the same about talking or asking questions. The risk in asking relatives is that it will stir up memories for them and for you. For some, thinking about the death and what it means to have lost a mother might be too much to handle emotionally. In the end, both you and they become upset.

Daughters are adamant that loss and grief in young people is valid and needs to be recognised. The need for consideration of bereaved children is embedded in the sentiments they express (with a degree of exasperation). Anne states:

> I don't think anybody ever stood back and thought, good God, these children have lost so much.

Theresa maintains:

> Adults don't think about the way it hits you like a ton of bricks when you are fourteen, fifteen or sixteen.

WISHFUL THINKING

When you are bereaved early in life, the yearning for your mother is ever-present. The days when you feel angry or jealous are the hardest to bear. If you observe other girls being ushered off to school with a kiss and a hug at their front door, you want your mother even more. As time goes on the feelings remain, as Abbey found:

> I feel envious of my friends and even my colleagues in work; most of them still have their mothers.

In order to survive the trauma, there are days of wishful thinking. A desire to turn the clock back and experience 'normality' or what other people have. Elena's words express the sentiments of many:

> I feel you would love it if you could turn back the clock. It is only when you can look back on it as an adult – you never had what was normal; you never had what other people had, but you had to go on.

Clare too wonders about the possibilities of what might have been – would her mum have pushed her to do things that her dad may not have done?

Like many other daughters, Mary longed to 'connect' with her mother. She said that she needed 'divine inspiration' in school and it motivated her to pray for her mother's assistance. While praying she became annoyed and 'fell out with God'. Her words to him were:

> Well look, if she's there with you, why don't you let her appear to me in a dream in some way.

The young Mary thought that if she concentrated hard enough while out walking, that her mother would talk to her and tell her what to do or why she had died. With a longing in her voice, Mary continues:

> I wish my mother hadn't died. I wish I could live my life over again with her being there. I'd love that to happen. I might have been better educated; we might have been all the more affectionate towards each other; we might have been better people.

Maggie compares her situation to those who are adopted:

> I remember people who were adopted and I thought, isn't that great how you can find out who your mother is; you could find her. She would be out there somewhere. You could find out and even if she wasn't the person you wanted her to be, at least you could physically see her. I think I missed that loss of physically seeing or having a sense of a presence, not having that at all.

Light-heartedness on Maggie's part does not mask her deep yearning for an opportunity to spend time or at least see her mother for an afternoon or a day. She says:

> An afternoon with her would do [laughter], just to get a sense of her; an afternoon or a day to have her totally, only with me, not a shared memory, just totally with me. And we would spend the time together and I'd ask her all the questions that I wanted to, almost like an adopted daughter finding her birth mother and spending the day with them. I might feel at the end of that day, God, I would have loved to have had her in my life.

However, Helen's view is that too much longing and pining may leave you with a sense of 'wishing your life away' if you dwelt too much on what might have been.

The early loss of a mother is a life-changing event that impacts on the quality of life for all the survivors. When a mother dies, everyone wants to protect the young. People worry about the effect the loss will have on the children, so a mother's history, life, illness and death is relegated to that of a 'closely guarded secret' within the family. Reflecting on the silence that prevails following the death of a mother and what it means not to be able to openly talk and discuss it, Alison is resolute that things need to change. She is firm and clear in her contention that:

There should be freedom not to forget.

2. 'YOUR WORST NIGHTMARE'

*I remember being at school and we were told, right, it's Mothering
Sunday and we are going to make Mother's Day cards, and that's
your worst nightmare if your mother is dead* – Lesley.

As a family embark on the future without a mother, there is little
knowledge of what lies ahead or what to expect. It is a time when
everything in life is in a state of upheaval, an unsettled, bleak
period for both children and adults. The changes that come about
can seem endless; nothing is the same anymore. Any sense of
security and comfort that existed is severely disrupted and, like the
rest of the family, bereaved daughters have much to cope with
emotionally. When children are already familiar with emotional
pain through the loss of their mother, the aftermath can be like
living in a 'nightmare'.

In the various environments that children are part of – home,
school or playtime with friends – difficulties can and do arise.
When they venture out into the unfamiliar surroundings of the
school room, children can face innumerable challenges on a day-to-
day or week-to-week basis. Learning to cope with an unknown,
uncertain world is a daunting and uneasy process for young
children. The child who is bereaved of a mother in early life is
already living in a state of emotional discomfort, overloaded by the
grief of the loss. In learning to cope and adjust to school, the
bereaved child faces the same difficulties as every other child, along
with the added burden that coping with a loss can bring.

As their lives unfold and they begin to experience life without
their mother, daughters realise that it is not only the loss of their

mother they have to contend with, it is also the consequences that stem from her loss. Here are some of the things that start to worry young children: when the loss is not known in school; when other children, who have not experienced the loss of a parent, make hurtful remarks; when a replacement mother figure comes along; when the phase of life called puberty is thrust upon them. In managing all of these situations, the feelings a bereaved child holds can intensify because they are bereaved. The loss becomes an indelible part of life because the reminders are ever-present; they crop up nearly on a daily basis. As daughters begin to explain their experiences in school, a mixed bag of positive and negative events emerge. If the loss is not known about, teachers are deprived of the opportunity to respond appropriately. In other instances, it is ignored or poorly managed. However, some teachers who know of the death respond warmly.

'THE TEACHER AUTOMATICALLY TOOK ON A ROLE'

When teachers were aware of the circumstances, some daughters found that they were sensitive to their needs. It made a tremendous difference to their experience of school when meaningful acts of kindness were offered, regardless of how small. Just as important, teachers were remembered for them. Liz appreciated the support provided by her teacher who gave her a little snack at lunchtime each day. As Liz explained, it was not only the kindness that was appreciated, it was the sensitive way in which it was delivered: as they would be dismissed for lunch the teacher would simply say, 'Liz, just a moment dear', and when the remainder of the class departed, she would receive her daily gift from the teacher. Ann grew up in the country and attended a small school, and when the death became known, there was help available:

> At the small local primary school, the teacher automatically took on a role because she knew your mum wasn't there. She would have helped with things. There would have been that network around.

As she speaks about her experience of school, Maude touchingly recalls her first day and the support shown to her by an insightful teacher:

> I remember the first day I went to school; I didn't want to go to school because my mother had just died and it was just a few days after, and they thought maybe I would be better in school. So I cried the whole way to school with my sister, who was five-and-a-half years older than me. My teacher was lovely – she was very old with beautiful white hair, and I just really loved her. She was a great person. She knew, and she said, 'I think we'll let you go in with your sister'. I went in with her for about a week and then I said I was alright and I'd go back to my own class, which I did.

'BEREAVEMENT WASN'T DISCUSSED IN SCHOOL'

Young daughters didn't know what to expect in school, but they hoped that the death of their mother would not be ignored, that it would be acknowledged and given recognition, particularly by teachers. But when the death and loss of a mother is not mentioned either at home or in school, there is little outlet for the child to express how they feel. Somehow, the silence that exists at home is compounded by a lack of acknowledgement in school.

'ACKNOWLEDGEMENT WOULD HAVE BEEN GREAT'

A sensitive response would have been welcomed, but as Kathleen discloses, 'Bereavement wasn't discussed in school at all'. Jennifer confirms that: 'There was absolutely no recognition, it just wasn't mentioned'. However, as Anne discovered, when teachers don't know that a death has occurred, they are unable to commiserate. Throughout Anne's secondary-level education, the death of her mother was not mentioned. However, when she spoke with her teacher in recent years she found out why. Her teacher explained to her: 'I didn't even know your mammy was dead. I went through the entire time of knowing you, not realising.'

Perhaps knowledge of the death could have made a difference to both the teacher and the child, but the lack of communication can be costly. Jennifer speaks stoically about her experience when she returned to school after the death of her mother:

> School was very unhelpful. My mother died in August and they made absolutely no reference to it in school, except one time the teacher asked who did the cooking in our house. There was no reference to it whatsoever; some kind of acknowledgement would have been great.

The need for a sensitive approach to the early bereaved seems to transcend all aspects of life in school. It is not only an acknowledgement of the death that is yearned for, but a need for consideration of the impact that the early loss of a mother has on the young mind. Mention of anything associated with the loss will impact very heavily on the child. This can include inadvertent comments (from teachers and peers), some of which may be innocently offered but are painfully received. For example, attempting to discipline a child with reference to their mother can result in distress and upset. The teacher who reprimands a bereaved child for stepping out of line (even for a minor transgression) with the comment, 'you wouldn't have done that if your mother was alive', may not realise the shock, anger, embarrassment and humiliation that is felt as a result of it. In turn, however, the anger felt at this remark may have induced the counter-attack, 'you wouldn't be treating me this way if she was'.

Maude was clear that when children make comments such as, 'It's awful that you have no mammy', no matter how well-meant they may be, they cause anguish and distress to a bereaved child. When her peers made such comments, Elena felt very hurt:

> When I was at school, some of the children did say to me, 'You haven't got any mother, your mam's dead'. You felt bad, you felt that bad.

Jennifer didn't get taunted at school but she was very aware that her brother did:

> Someone teased him for not having a mother, for his mother dying.

In school, there may be little escape from other children's hurtful remarks. Not having experienced the loss of a parent can impair other children's appreciation of the hurt and distress that their remarks can cause. It might also be difficult for a bereaved child in school to find a peer that they can relate to or who can relate to them, unless another pupil had also experienced the trauma of loss.

TOUCHUNG A RAW NERVE

In the course of their duties, teachers set tasks for pupils to meet the demands of the curriculum and to help enrich the development of their young protégés. No matter how they feel about the task that is proposed, children usually comply. However, teachers (even when they know of the death) may not suspect that certain tasks can impact profoundly on children. In an attempt to be inclusive, the teacher may inadvertently add to the nightmare. At the opening of this chapter, Lesley spoke about the task of making a Mother's Day card, a universally standard project in the classroom setting. She continues:

> There was another girl in the class whose mother had died as well. We were called up and asked if there was anybody we could make our Mother's Day cards for, like a granny, and I thought, how inconsiderate – what kind of person would do that to a child? And what could you do? You were the pupil and this was the teacher and you just had to get on with it.

The happy occasion of being presented with a prize can also turn into a nightmare, when, in front of the entire staff and pupils of the school the head teacher remarks that you are 'going to go out shopping with your mother to spend it all at the weekend'. From the child's perspective, this can be an embarrassing and humiliating experience, especially when she realises that teachers and friends know that her mother has died. But when teachers are not informed of a death, they are not given the opportunity to react in an appropriate manner. Anne recalls an incident in school when a visiting science teacher came to take the class. She recaptures the scene:

> Myself and a friend were sitting at the end of a table in the science lab and we were sort of chatting. He turned around to me and said, 'You, Anne, your mother wrote to me and said that she wanted me to separate you two'. Everybody in the class went 'ooohh'. I got so upset, I ran out, and he was so upset when he heard. He was just devastated that he had said that to me and he was just so apologetic.

In coping with the loss of a mother, young children are dealing with many thoughts and feelings that may disrupt their ability to concentrate in class. Even if a child has friends, is never in trouble and seems to be doing well, they may (inwardly) detest school. It can become an intolerable place that is hated and loathed. The anxiety that a child feels can be invisible to others and their behaviour can change completely. Liz recalls that she was 'a difficult child at school but related to one or two of the teachers, who were kind', one of whom reminded her of a favourite aunt. During her early education in the 1970s, Kathleen said that her behaviour 'just turned the other way' when she got into trouble and was slapped by the teacher. It was in looking back she realised that, at the time, she didn't fully understand what was happening to her:

> For me to get slapped was just appalling; one of the best behaved children the whole way up, and our family had been really respected in the school. It was just a big catastrophe for me. I couldn't understand it, I didn't even know why I was behaving that way. I wasn't even aware that I was behaving differently but obviously something had gone wrong, you know, when I look back on it.

The lack of sensitive handling of bereaved children led daughters to conclude that teachers weren't taught how to respond to loss and bereavement in school. The compassion and understanding that they craved was missing. While struggling to cope mentally and emotionally with the death of their mother, some daughters endured physical and mental abuse and humiliation, sometimes in front of other pupils. Some who were educated in earlier decades (before legislation relating to the management of children in school changed) gave heart-rending descriptions that illustrate the extremely difficult encounters they experienced.

TEACHERS 'WEREN'T EDUCATED' ON THOSE ISSUES

Remembering and recalling her story was visibly difficult for Louise; like all the daughters who shared their experiences of early bereavement, her determination to raise awareness and insight surpassed the difficulty of expressing her feelings:

> I had a lot of anxiety inside, even as a young child. In primary school I was so anxious that, for example, when the class work was given to me I ended up getting all the sums wrong and I would be put standing in the corner for ages and getting slapped. I always felt I had no-one there to advise me or guide me.

> The teachers in those days weren't educated on those issues. Instead of showing a little bit of compassion ... I remember, because I was left-handed I would use a knife on this side [left] and a fork on this side [right] and still do. I used to get physically pulled out of the chair by the teacher and slapped about the head. He called me 'cach-handed'. He used to make me sit with the knife and fork in front of the other pupils and I used to have to try to eat and he would slap me every time I dropped it. I just felt loneliness; loneliness all the time. I kept pining for my own mother and I kept thinking, why did she die, why isn't she here?

It was the daughters' view that through training, teachers would help to develop their understanding of the range of symptoms that bereaved children can experience. Enhanced understanding would enable teachers to 'read' the pupil's symptoms or behaviour in the classroom and respond appropriately, not punitively. The symptoms manifested in the bereaved child's behaviour would then be recognised and responded to with sensitivity and understanding.

In school, daughters who have been bereaved usually wish to avoid any discussion of the death with their peers. 'I didn't want to talk about it, I just wanted to keep it all to myself,' explains Maude. It can be a form of self-protection, a way of not being regarded as different from others. However, if a child doesn't want to talk, this presents a dilemma to the teacher who sees and understands the situation and wants to help. So what is a teacher to do in this situation? Kathleen, being sensitive to those in pain, quickly spots a change in young children under her care in the classroom. She would immediately notice and identify the indicators that all is not well. It could be a child who is bereaved through death or when the family splits up, but when a child is 'suffering' it is exhibited in their behaviour and the quality of their school work. Kathleen's solution is to engage with the child, find out what is going on and try to help:

> I would focus on them and try and do a lot of work for their self-esteem, circle-time work and stuff like that, because I could see them suffering. I would be aware that their work and their behaviour would suffer. You would notice when you're with a child for two years what would happen. I'd be with them for six or seven years and I would notice things happening and you would zoom in there quick. You are not always told, but even if you are not told, you notice when a child's behaviour changes anyway, and then you try and find out what has caused it.

While some may require training in bereavement, loss and grief to identify the signs and signals you need to watch out for in the classroom, Kathleen was consciously aware of the signs that said something was wrong. Thankfully, teachers are given more help, guidance and training these days on how to respond to a grieving child. Not everyone has the confidence to react and manage a child in distress. But if educators understand and appreciate what a child may be going through, they are best placed to offer the help and support the child needs to get through a very critical period in life. Some schools have policies and procedures in place that staff can use as a guide, to provide a foundation on which loss and grief can be managed when it occurs. This is good because daughters are clear that they would prefer the school to acknowledge loss rather than ignore it. In that case, if schools are better equipped to help a child, there is hope that a more positive outcome is possible for all concerned.

'NO PUSH' TOWARDS AN EDUCATION

There is little that is normal in the months and years that extend beyond the death of a mother. The grief of the loss is consuming for children and adults. The things in life that perhaps had flown along reasonably well before the death are now overshadowed and distorted by the loss.

In the aftermath of a mother's death, the circumstances at home reduce the likelihood of schooling and education taking precedence, especially in the unsettled years following the death. Daughters were unanimous that the gap created by the death of their mother impacted strongly on their educational journey. The loss, it seems, diminished their chances of being encouraged and supported through school. Fathers, carers and older siblings enlisted the help of the children to take on additional roles and other duties. However, inheriting other roles interfered with schooling. Mary, who was six when her mother died in childbirth, found that growing up in the 1940s brought with it additional pressures:

> We weren't educated because we had so much to do – we had to come home and start into the work.

She goes on to say:

> I have learned more since I left school than I did at school. I feel that had my mother been living, I would have been better educated because I wouldn't have had as much to do. Being only six, and right through to fourteen, everything had to be done because the other children had to be brought up and looked after.

In the decades of the 1960s and 1970s, daughters like Elizabeth had similar challenges in their educational journey:

> I think, in hindsight, we missed out on a lot because Daddy was a farmer and we had nobody to give us a wee push there to keep on going at school. When we would come home from school you had to start into the work. When it came to the evening, we had a tilly lamp and you could hardly see the books. Half the time things were thrown away and I know that our education wasn't up to much. There was nobody there to give you the push.

In the end, Elizabeth says, school was abandoned in order to earn a living. Feeling that she had no push within herself or from others, Theresa also resigned herself to leaving school and seeking a job. She recalls how other duties interrupted her attempts to do homework:

> You go to your lessons and somebody would be saying, 'Are you not making tea?' You never got any peace, you never got your head down. You were up and down, up and down, up and down. I was unsettled and there was no push at all, no push, and I didn't have enough push in myself. I just left school then and got a job.

Many daughters reported that they felt acutely the lack of push that Theresa describes. Alison was unwavering in her conviction that things would have been different if her mother hadn't died:

> I left school just after doing my O-levels. I wanted to stay on but there wasn't that push. I know for a fact that if my mother had been alive I would have stayed at school and done A-levels and maybe gone to university.

It was the opportunity to go to university that Karen also felt 'deprived of', especially when other family members attended, while Joanna spoke wistfully of her desire for somebody to push her on in her education and tell her when she was doing well.

As daughters viewed it, it was the *gap* created by the loss of their mother that caused their education to suffer. The driving force, their mother, the central source of support and encouragement, was gone and this now impacted on the daughters' motivation to take the initiative towards schoolwork. It was as if the role was vacated and not taken over by others. Daughters felt that things would have been different if their mother had been there, but felt also that they did not have the ability to push themselves. However, those who were ambitious and keen to pursue their education were angry when they were met with opposition.

LACK OF SUPPORT FOR DAUGHTERS' FURTHER EDUCATION

In speaking about the resistance they met in relation to their desire to progress in their education, daughters spoke clearly and intensely. Sometimes objections to further education were financially driven: 'I'll not be paying, we can hardly afford a loaf'.

However, Pauline said that she loved learning and if she had been given the chance, she mightn't have left school at sixteen with 'nothing, not one exam'. Joanna found that her father disagreed with the route she had chosen:

> *The course I wanted to do wasn't what my dad wanted me to do, so he didn't pay for my degree in university.*

Being denied her education caused Liz to feel resentful. She explained that when the money was available from another source her father 'stood firm and would not move.

> *So I was denied my grammar school education. And I was really, really disappointed, devastated. I was, as a child, devastated.*

Perhaps, from the perspective of a bereaved child, learning could be a way of coping in the aftermath of the loss. A daughter having lost out on the opportunity for a future with her mother did not want to lose out on the opportunity for learning.

And as the years unfolded, puberty hit! Entering puberty is a time when the young can have personal worries that they need to share with someone. It is a time when the gap created by the loss seems to expand and become even more apparent. Trying to navigate the perplexing adolescent years without their mother left daughters searching for someone to talk to, someone who could answer their questions and clear up the confusion about the facts of life.

PUBERTY: 'I WOULD HAVE LIKED SOMEONE TO TALK TO'
Puberty is an important developmental phase in the lives of the young. At this time of significant change and growth, daughters found themselves in a kind of information limbo and struggling to know how to cope. There was agreement that fathers didn't talk to children about sex; however, some, like Maude, had an older sister who explaind things:

> My father wouldn't talk about sex. Probably no man talked to their children about it, you know. But having no mother, it was left. Luckily, the eldest was eighteen so she was able to talk; you looked on her as a mother.

As the oldest in the house, however, Elaine found it tough-going when puberty came along. She said that she would have liked someone to talk to, 'especially someone who won't get totally embarrassed', because there are still questions that needed to be asked. For others, being left in the dark without information led to annoyance that was conveyed in the words: 'Nobody ever thought that they better speak to these girls'.

Pauline recalls that while household duties were taught, sex education was avoided:

> All these women around were telling us how to do the washing and
> telling us how to iron, and not one of them telling us about periods
> and what to get and where to go. Not one of them telling us anything,
> maybe only that you would need a bra.

In the absence of a mother or anyone else to talk to, friends became
an important source of help and support for Joanna:

> Not having anybody, nobody, you could talk to about boys – it was
> your friends who were counsellors.

To help them understand and cope with the facts of life as they
were growing up, daughters turned to older sisters; in some cases a
brother, close friends or a friend's mother became sources of
support and help. But it irritated Pauline that she had to seek
information on the street to alleviate the confusion when her sister
got her first period and thought she was going to die:

> I went out to the street to see what I could find out. I asked my
> friend's mother and she said, 'Sit down and I'll tell you'. Why
> couldn't somebody else have done that?

Without someone she felt she could turn to, Kathleen told no-one
when her first period arrived in the first year of secondary school.
Coping on her own presented her with several difficulties (including
making her own sanitary wear), but she doesn't blame her family for
not noticing her dilemma; as she explains philosophically, 'they were
older and they had their own lives to lead'.

The legacy of the loss of a mother was beginning to impact on
different aspects of young daughters' lives. The journey was
characterised by silence, and most 'felt restricted in talking openly'
about it. A similar shadow of silence arched over the growing-up
years in which daughters experienced loneliness in the absence of
their mother. The conviction was that, had she been there, her
presence would have influenced the quality of their lives.

In subsequent years, circumstances in which some daughters
were cared for and looked after underwent major changes. In a

number of cases, daughters remained with their father (and siblings), while others were reared away from the family home with grandparents or aunts and uncles. The death of their mother had 'changed the whole course of everything' and the introduction of a new mother figure through remarriage, partnership or aunts in the family circle 'turned life upside down'. The alteration in family structure was a considerable re-adjustment for both young children and adults. In all, nine of the twenty-six daughters who shared their experiences were reared with a replacement mother figure.

Different rules, different attitude, different means of discipline

When daughters spoke about their lives beyond the death of their mother, their accounts of the new family environment were sometimes accompanied by nervous laughter and tears. Those who lived in new circumstances with a replacement mother figure reported with remarkable consistency how the adjustment took its toll on their emotional, physical and mental health. There were those, too, who were philosophical in their outlook and then some, like Alison, whose new life began optimistically. At the outset, Alison says she and her siblings were excited about 'having a new mum'. However, as time went on, when new rules were enforced around friends, mealtimes, bedtimes and pocket money, it made home feel like a place that was no longer free; it was strict and restrictive.

While Joanna had to 'prime herself' by holding her breath and counting to three before she was able to ask for anything, she expressed sympathy as she reflected on the role her stepmother had undertaken:

> I suppose it couldn't have been easy for her. She was working full-time, she had come into a family with four stepchildren. So I can sympathise if I try to imagine myself in the same situation.

With hindsight, Joanna appreciated the enormity of stepping into someone else's shoes to rear their children.

Mary B adopted a similar attitude to her situation. She explained that her relationship with her stepmother developed gradually (when her father remarried three years after the death):

> When I was ten my father married again so I had a stepmother who came out of town, and she did not have an easy life. My stepmother came into that house with two stepchildren; nobody would do it nowadays.

While there were decisions that Mary B 'didn't particularly like' and that her brother might have objected to, she tried to accept that they were being done for the right reasons. However, it was the opportunity to get involved in the upbringing of her step-siblings that helped to forge 'a very good relationship' in the long run. Being included helped in the bonding process.

It is tremendously difficult for a child to move on and adjust to new arrangements within the household when the death and loss of a mother is not acknowledged or discussed. The young have a myriad of feelings and reactions to cope with and daughters didn't understand all of what was going on inside of them, but they knew it was like being a 'different person in a different state'. They have not yet grieved the death and loss of their natural mother, and when someone attempts to replace her, the child, still raw from the loss, can be resentful.

Children are acutely aware and sensitive in situations where other children are managed differently or offered opportunities that they are denied. In these situations, the young desire fairness and equality. However, it was the 'different rules, different attitude, and different means' of discipline that applied throughout their upbringing that daughters deeply regretted. Being treated 'totally different' from step-siblings was deeply hurtful and caused inner resentment.

The way in which a distinction was made between daughters and their step-brothers and/or sisters was succinctly described. For example, compared to their step-brothers and/or sisters, much more was expected of daughters and their siblings in their childhood years in terms of the amount of housework and chores undertaken. In some cases, if the work was not done correctly they would be penalised; this might mean being locked in the kitchen because they hadn't washed and dried the dishes and put them away in ten minutes. Differences also emerged in terms of opportunities afforded to family members; for example, music lessons and driving lessons were denied to the bereaved children in some cases.

Some daughters graphically illustrated the intolerable cruelty and abuse they had to live through and endure for many years. They were adamant that their stories should be shared so that others would understand the depth and breadth of the emotional and physical abuse they experienced in their growing-up years. At times, their accounts were clear and frank, and left little to the imagination.

Helen's view is that everything stemmed from the fact that she lost her mother when she was three-and-a-half years old. As she exclaimed, she was beaten and 'constantly put down' throughout her childhood. Liz summarised the years of being 'beaten regularly' and treated differently as 'a very distressing period of time'. It was the shock of being beaten and trying to understand why it was happening that was so difficult to comprehend, because at first Liz had been treated with love and kindness by her replacement 'mother'. At the age of six months she went to live with her uncle and his first wife, who were very good to her. Sadly, however, she suffered the loss of her new 'mother' when she was two. Her replacement 'mother', Auntie Jessie, was a very kind and loving housekeeper that she remembered fondly. But it was when her uncle remarried that things took a turn for the worse. She goes on to explain what her life was like at the time:

The first time that she was physical towards me I just couldn't understand what had happened. I couldn't believe it. So I waited for uncle [name] to come home and I said, 'She beat me'. And he said, 'Why did she beat you?' and I had no answer for him. So I was beaten the next day because I told. I was hammered and told under no circumstances ever, ever, ever again to tell him if she touched me: 'If you tell you'll get beaten twice as hard for having told.' So, like the majority of children in that situation, I didn't tell him. However, he suspected. There were red eyes when he came home because I was beaten regularly and he would say to me, 'Have you been beaten?' 'No no,' I said, 'no, no'. He said, 'You look as if you were crying', and I pretended to sniffle and cough and say, 'I have a cold'. But I know that he knew that I was beaten and I know that it caused trouble in the house.

It was just the trauma of it all. I just couldn't understand why I had been beaten. She was an unkind person; she was very devoted to her own daughter, but she was definitely not devoted to me. I suffered really, really badly. I used to linger behind when we would walk down the street. She would have her daughter by the hand and I would be walking, looking down at the ground in front of me with a doleful face. She used to say, 'Come on humpy, come on humpy'.

Liz was resolute that having the 'stuffing knocked out' of her was bound to have an effect. In fact, she was sure that for anyone enduring the same experience, it was bound to affect self-esteem and bound to affect feelings of self-worth. Therefore, Liz attributed the physical abuse and upbringing rather than the loss of her mother who had died when she was five months old to any loss of self-esteem or loss of confidence that she experienced.

Others like Louise suffered in their newly inherited life. She (nervously) provides a graphic account of her experience growing up, which she summed up as 'horrendous psychological torture':

The situation at home just became very abusive with my stepmother and my father. There were a lot of beatings, just horrendous psychological torture [laughs nervously], and when that was going on I clung to the thought of my own mother. I wished she was here and asked why did she die, and it made me more obsessive, thinking about her.

As she continues, it clearly takes courage for Louise to reveal that she was being 'hit' right up to the age of twenty-three, for example for opening the fridge door to see what was there to eat after returning from professional work:

I still had a feeling of relief actually a couple of weeks after she died because I was able to open the fridge door without getting thumped. She still hit me when I would have been twenty-two, twenty-three. It was about the year before she died, that was the last time she hit me.

In an account that was delivered with much emotion, Elaine wanted to alert others to the predicament that she found herself in when her father remarried. It was not only the adjustment to a new mother figure that was extremely difficult for her and her siblings, but also the trauma of abuse imposed on the family by a male step-relative (who was introduced to the family through her father's second marriage). The events caused Elaine to experience a psychological breakdown in the end. She begins her account by explaining that her stepmother was initially her nanny and continues with an open assessment of her life at the time:

The mother of my four younger brothers and sisters, a very nasty piece of work, came on the scene as our nanny. Of course, Dad and her fell in love and then life was absolutely shit after that, absolutely awful, just terrible [very emotional at this point]. I really lost my temper with my dad one night and I accused him of causing a lot of trouble by bringing [name] into the house. She was an absolutely awful, very, very, mixed-up person. She used to have us tortured.

Daughters were not only bereaved of their natural mother, some had to live a life filled with fear and anguish in a climate of cruelty and abuse that impacted profoundly on them. Circumstances were such that forming a relationship or attempting to accept their new mother as a replacement was going to be extremely difficult due to the beatings and cruelty.

REARED AWAY FROM THE FAMILY HOME WITH OTHER FAMILY RELATIVES

Five daughters were reared away from home with aunts and uncles or grandparents. The decision to have the daughters raised elsewhere was based on their age at the time of the death; two were five months old, another two weeks. In another case, outlined in the first chapter, a mother's death meant the loss of a father figure (her mother's partner) and the extended family relocated the children to be raised with an aunt and uncle. Another daughter and her siblings were reared with her maternal grandparents as her father and mother were separated prior to the death.

Being reared away from the family home brought with it strong and sometimes complex feelings for daughters. The opportunity for bonding was affected by the separation, as Maggie found. Raised by her maternal grandparents following the death of her mother when she was five months old, Maggie reported that she had a 'full' life during her upbringing; however, she was envious of her siblings. She had a feeling of being alone, not being part of the family unit:

I also remember being very lonely and feeling like I was an only child.

Being reared away from the family took its toll on the bonding process. Daughters raised separately were without the opportunity for a shared journey through loss and grief with their siblings. They experienced feelings of not belonging, of distance, loneliness, jealousy and uncertainty. There was the perception that siblings reared together were a 'unit' and not being 'part of them' was difficult. However, as daughters discovered, being reared together did not necessarily promote bonding. When it was noted (in the focus group discussion) that the bonding process was affected by being separated from the family and reared elsewhere, Liz revealed that even though the other siblings in her family had been reared together, 'they didn't bond':

> I have hardly any bonding with my brothers and sisters. I personally don't feel any emotional ties to any of them. There is no acrimony or anything like that, it might be like distant cousins. We send Christmas cards to each other and that's it. My two brothers and two sisters are basically strangers. I've just had no experience of bonding.

The sensitivity that children can feel around the issue of upbringing is illustrated in Elena's account. Being initially reared with her brother at the home of their paternal uncle and then later separated gave rise to doubts and questions that remain unresolved in her mind at the time of the interview. After a number of years, Elena's father took her brother back to be reared in the family home. She observed that her father had always 'leaned' towards her brother, and given that her mother died a few weeks after giving birth to her, Elena questioned whether this was due to the fact that he blamed her for 'wrecking the home'. The 'silence' that existed and the lack of explanation of events meant that several years later, insecurities and questions remain unanswered:

> I was reared with my aunt and uncle. They worked very hard, there was no money, no government money like now. We were just reared on the farm. My uncle was very good because he took another man's two children and reared them. Never got anything for it, he did it himself and, as I say, he reared us off the farm. We would have worked too but then my brother went to Daddy and I was there on my own.

COPING AND NOT COPING IN THE 'NIGHTMARE'

Coping in the aftermath of the loss was not easy. It was not only the change to the tone and texture of family life brought about by the death that fuelled daughters' frustration as we have seen, it was also the experiences embedded in school life, throughout puberty, being raised with a replacement mother figure and raised away from the family home that took a toll.

Daughters wanted to explain their psychological reactions to the loss but they also wanted to talk about their ways of coping. The most important thing for daughters was to keep their deceased mother's memory alive – to retain a sense of closeness or 'connection', including through physical momentos that were meaningful and representative of their mother. For example, the 'taste' of a creamy lipstick that was worn by her mother brings comfort to Abbey and her sisters:

> One memory that does stick in my mind and even for my other two sisters is the taste of her lipstick. It's quite a rich sort of taste, a creamy taste that reminds me of Mummy. So that memory is still very, very strong.

'I DID TERRIBLE THINGS AS A TEENAGER'

Some struggled, however, with their own internal changes in attitude; it felt like a 'rebellion' was going on inside of them against the death and loss *and* the changes that it brought. For example, when Pauline lost her mother at the age of eight, she struggled to make sense of her life and to retain her health. Suffering from a very early age with migraines and a feeling of being stuck in the 'black hole' of depression, Pauline lashed out at the world:

> I did terrible things as a teenager, but looking back, it was attention-seeking behaviour. I put windows in with my fist and I got attention, negative or otherwise. I got arrested for shoplifting – that was the best attention I got of the whole lot. I ended up getting a social worker and she was great. She was grand because you could bounce things off her;

you would have come out of a session feeling you could hit the road again. She never came to the house, it was really at school she came to talk to me. When I was fourteen I took an overdose of tablets. You hear people talking about this black hole and you can't get out of it. For me, that is very real.

While Pauline and Louise experienced early depression, Helen E and Jennifer developed eating disorders in their teenage years and Kathleen spoke about a concealed pregnancy in her late teens. Louise had tried everything, including visits to her doctor, to get help for the anxiety and depression she felt, with little success. She feels strongly that help should have been at hand:

I remember when I was a teenager going to the doctor and begging him to give me something. I was so anxious, so fearful of the beatings and all. I remember he said at the time, 'No, you are not allowed them'. Looking back then too, I wish the doctor had realised that someone coming in at that age of fifteen/fourteen, this isn't right, and maybe he should have referred me somewhere, got me help. Around that same time I started having seizures as well and I was never ever taken [to the doctor] as a child. I used to collapse in school in epileptic seizures. Now I know you can get them through chronic stress. That went on for about two years. I do feel that this has something to do with all that stress throughout my life, it triggered it.

You have no peace, you don't realise it, but you have no peace and you are tormented with the bereavement and I was tormented by the abuse and then the psychological anxiety and depression of it. It is basically searching for peace all the time – whether that means going to social workers or getting them involved or teachers or counselling – something to bring peace to people like me.

A significant ritual that brought Louise a sense of safety and security remained part of her life throughout her growing-up years. She explains:

I would carry a small photograph of her around constantly and if I forgot it, and this happened right up until I was in [name of profession], I would have to go back to the house to find it. I didn't feel safe and I didn't feel secure without it.

WRITING POEMS AND SHORT STORIES

Louise tried to combat her depression by writing poems about her mother and about her life:

I have always written poems and I read quite a lot. Looking back it was escapism; it was a way of focusing on something else as opposed to everything that happened. Reading a lot and educating myself was one way to cope with it.

Like Louise, Dara found solace in writing (as a way of remembering). She explained:

I have written poetry and short stories just about our family, anything I can remember about Mammy and all of us.

For Elaine there were many reasons to 'escape' and reading was her chosen method:

I would have read an awful lot. We would have taken ourselves off for the day once you got your chores done. I would have just thought – climb into the tree house and read. I would have done that all alone. I don't know whether it was a deliberate way of isolating yourself.

Mary B admitted that she 'spent half of her life up a tree in the summer reading a book'. This was partly to avoid chores on the farm that she hated, so she got herself 'out of sight'. She went on to explain that herself and her brother supported each other:

You learnt ways and means of looking after yourself. But you never complained, it never occurred to us. And if we were annoyed or hurt about something, we consoled each other. We tended to be running around the farm or cycling around the country or reading a book. I don't know what I would have done without reading; even now I could spend hours on my own. I don't miss company as long as I have a book.

'I STARTED BED-WETTING'

Maureen very courageously shared her 'nightmare' that had a profound and long-lasting effect on her life:

> After my mother died I started bed-wetting and I had an awful time then because I was so self-conscious of it. I couldn't seem to get control of my bladder. I remember going to boarding school – in those days there were no secondary schools, so you had to get a scholarship to go to a boarding school.
>
> I got a scholarship to go to this school, and from lying in wet beds probably at home as well and in boarding school I ended up getting rheumatic fever twice and I nearly died once. That left me with a damaged heart and three bad valves – one of them was replaced a few years ago. So that really all came from the rheumatic fever, from my bed-wetting.
>
> I was too ashamed to mention it. I used to be mortified about it but I had no control over it, and then it stopped, miraculously. This old nun said to me one day – she knew I was very upset – 'Why don't you say a prayer to the holy souls to wake you up because they are awake all night'. I did and from that day to this I never have bed-wet. Maybe it was a belief that I could stop, I don't know. From that day to this I never looked back but it has really impacted on my whole life since then.

'I WAS VIRTUALLY ANOREXIC'

The experience of an eating disorder occurred when some young daughters became 'obsessed' or 'conscious' of their weight; it was a time of 'punishment through food' and 'a lack of confidence'. Jennifer connected the anorexia (that was sustained until she was twenty-eight) with the death of her mother; she was convinced too that it took its 'toll mentally' because she felt depressed:

> I was virtually anorexic, probably throughout my teens until I reached the age of twenty-eight, and then, for some reason, it just stopped – this idea of punishing myself through food or not eating. I was very conscious

of my weight and thinking I was overweight. I was always baking and I had this idea that your worth was about being able to give people food, to buy food and all the rest of it. I think I was a bit mixed-up around all that. I definitely had tendencies towards bulimia as well.

Helen E was 'very ill' with anorexia during her teenage years but remains uncertain if there is a link with it and the loss of her mother. She revealed that she was diagnosed when she was seventeen at a time (the 1970s) when anorexia was less well understood:

Because my weight was so low I remember I had to go into [name of specialised hospital]. I remember sitting for a long time talking to a specialist. He said to me, 'I don't think you are anorexic', and he sent me home. I know that I went on a diet; I know that I became obsessed about my weight; I know that my weight dropped dramatically. I know that I was ill, very ill; I was obsessed with losing weight. I don't know how I came out of it and I don't know if it was linked to the loss of my mother.

'I HAD A CONCEALED PREGNANCY'

Until she went into labour, no-one knew that Kathleen was pregnant at the age of twenty-two. Even though her sisters were available as possible confidantes, she endured the pregnancy in isolation: 'Not another person in this world knew that I was pregnant.' It was a time when she felt isolated and missed her mother's support. When her baby daughter arrived and she met her future husband, 'things improved remarkably' for Kathleen. Her poignant account illustrates the devastation brought about by the loss of a mother and the brave attempt to survive and make life better:

I went to university and I got my degree and then I did [professional training] after that and came home. I had a concealed pregnancy. I had a lot of loneliness in my life. I would have loved to have had a mother to confide in and to talk to, and I didn't tell one person that I was pregnant, not even my best friend. I was living with my sisters at the time and I went into my sister's bedroom and I said, 'Look, I'm pregnant and I'm in labour'.

I didn't have a great relationship with the father anyway. But I believe that if I'd had Mammy there it would have been different, it would have been totally different. Then the relationship didn't last, it wasn't good anyway, he wasn't interested in my little girl, he just wasn't and that fell apart, and until [name of husband] came along, it was just a disaster really but then everything was great. I must say from the time Mammy died right up until [name of daughter] was born, I wasn't a happy person, I really wasn't.

Daughters' lives had changed radically. During their growing-up years, there was little opportunity for a shared process of mourning and grieving within their families. Not only had they to cope with the untimely death of their mother, they faced further trauma and challenges with little help and support. The strength shown by daughters in coping with adversity was evident in their meaningful efforts to survive. Despite the fact that their bereaved status was given little acknowledgement and they were essentially disempowered in their loss, they found ways of coping and developing resilience. Mary B reminded us, 'You learnt ways and means of looking after yourself'.

3. 'DIGGING FOR INFORMATION'

Because it was a closely guarded family secret it was very hard to get any information at all about who she was, any sort of background information. I thought I would try a little bit of digging for information. At that stage we had no photographs, we didn't know the date of death, we didn't know where the grave was, we really didn't know anything at all, and finding out became important – Helen.

In many households, the history of the family can often be accessed through conversations, photographs and other memorabilia, which help things to fall into place, to be understood. Those of us who have not had to search for meaning and understanding of the family history may not fully appreciate how important it was to the early bereaved to *know* something of their family. We may take for granted what in essence was a struggle for daughters. They craved knowledge about their mother, but the challenge they faced was to find ways to excavate information that could help them to form that much needed 'picture'. Even if the quantity of information was the bare minimum, it was finding the 'little bits and pieces' that was important to daughters thirsty for knowledge. However, breaking through the barrier of the 'closely guarded family secret' at times required bravery and sometimes a willingness to take risks.

The extract from Helen's testimony above is telling, deeply touching, and shocking. But in essence her words summarise the experiences of many in the study and perhaps many beyond. The enshrinement of a mother's history, life, illness and death into a 'closely guarded family secret' was a common feature of life as daughters grew up. Even in their adult years, much remained unknown about their mothers. What other people may not have realised was that the foundation of silence that existed to protect the children in their formative years left them in a kind of information limbo. As Ann said:

I didn't know my mother, I didn't know her personality, I didn't know what she was like.

The chasm that formed around conversations about deceased mothers seemed to expand rather than retract as time went on. Opening up the subject became more, not less, difficult. It was a tough barrier to break through but daughters, more curious as they got older, were determined to find out more. To break the silence, the 'digging' for information began and it took many forms (including a visit to a hypnotist!). Here we take time to explore what it was like for daughters to begin the process of discovery; what it was like for them to unearth snippets or large chunks of information about their mothers, and how the process of 'digging' and discovering impacted on them psychologically. We also consider the plight of those who knew where to access information but were still afraid to do so (at the time of the interview).

In the case where family life is not over-shadowed by death, it could be assumed (for the sake of argument) that the likes and dislikes of family members, their personality traits, or who resembles who are more open for debate and discussion. When there are no limitations placed on the topic, everyone may feel more relaxed about pitching in with their views and opinions; sometimes the 'truth' is achieved through good-humoured discussions or banter, sometimes through more meaningful dialogue. In such deliberations, we may not always like what we hear, but in a way the wrangling over which of our parents or ancestors we take after, the facial features or mannerisms that we have inherited, helped us to form our identity and to know who we were/who we are. Such experiences contrasted powerfully with those of the early bereaved.

Daughters didn't have the opportunity to develop a sense of themselves through their mother, the person who was or could have been their role model. In our society, the mother is regarded as the female figurehead that daughters observe and emulate; the person they are tied to biologically, mentally and emotionally. When, as in the case of the twenty-six daughters in the study, their mother died in those early years when identities were beginning to be formed, the loss of her impacted profoundly. Those who were very young at the time of the death barely knew her or remembered her at all; others had longer with her but there was not enough time to get to know her very well. Essentially, the person that they could have related to or identified with most had died and, without her, the daughter's psychological growth and development suffered. What made it especially hard for the children was that their mother became a closed subject within the household – it was almost as if she never existed. This did not help them to get a sense of who she was or give them a chance to 'retain' her in their lives so that in knowing something of her, they might know and understand themselves better. That is, in order to understand who *they were*, they needed to have a sense of who *she was* in their minds. In the aftermath of the loss, without a chance to build a picture of her through inherited knowledge, the process of rebuilding or restoring their identities was going to be severely disrupted. Without 'knowing' her, daughters struggled to know themselves.

But in the shadow of the loss, everyone was suffering; the adults were unable, for the most part, to assist daughters in their attempts to mentally reconstruct their mother's life, illness and death. Seeking knowledge through questions was futile. As we read in the first chapter, the silence that surrounded the loss made it nearly impossible for daughters to raise the topic or ask questions (in case they upset the adults). However, Theresa and others in the study recognised and highlighted that bereaved husbands/partners/fathers need help and support, although they may not always seek it:

> Men need a lot of support to deal with the children and the loss of their partner.

'RELATIVES CREATED MEMORIES'

However, not everyone was kept totally in the dark. Over the years, there were a few who had sources of information such as maternal aunts and maternal grandmothers. In Patricia's words, 'youngsters need to know'. She went on to say: 'While my father didn't speak a lot about it, our auntie created memories for us'. The opportunity to find out more was welcomed, but even in these cases, daughters realised as life went on that there was still a lot they didn't know. For example, Patricia later confirmed that it was only in the previous year (her fortieth) that she had found out the date of her mother's birthday.

Left motherless, without their nurturer and role model, daughters felt adrift in their developing years. Their anchor was gone and they were not in possession of the knowledge that might have helped them to piece together a chronology of their mothers' lives, histories and deaths. The chance to 'know' the woman who was their mother had rarely been presented to them, with the exception of a few like Dara, who, in the years that followed, was 'filled in' about her mother by one of her mother's cousins. She appreciated their efforts and found the insights they provided to be 'really, really interesting'. However, with the lack of information and other physical artefacts such as photographs, some daughters (especially those who were very young when she died) had many unanswered questions: do I look like my mother? Have I the same nature or personality as she had? The answers to some fundamental questions also remained unknown: when did she die? Where was she buried?

Despite the lack of assistance or support, daughters were determined to delve into their mothers' histories to help them formulate an image or 'picture' of her. Making sense of things was virtually impossible until this was achieved. They had been starved of information for a long time, and as their lives unfolded the deep desire to know more became stronger and stronger. It was as if they had waited long enough and they were ready to absorb any information that came their way. The knowledge they lacked now became vital – 'knowing' became important, urgent, essential. It was determination that fuelled the efforts of some to dig for information.

THE NEED TO KNOW MORE

One of the central messages contained in the testimonies was that daughters wanted to be 'included' rather than 'shut out'. Like many others, Helen E was clear that things could have been managed differently:

> I would have liked to have known much more about her than I did, to have been told what was happening when she died.

But she was equally clear that she didn't blame anyone and that, in her view, adults did the best they could at the time.

Many daughters referred in different ways to the sense that their mother was a 'closed subject' and that her memory was not 'alive' within the household. It was the lack of knowledge or any artefacts that precipitated Louise's search for her mother's grave:

> Nothing had ever been explained to me about my mother dying and never was, right up until I was about nineteen. I started to find out the background and everything about her. There were never any photographs about the house or anything to keep her memory alive.

When the grave was eventually discovered, Louise began attending it 'obsessively' and these visits became an important but 'secret' feature of her life:

> *When I got a bit older I started obsessively going to her grave. I used*
> *to go around the cemetery trying to find her grave. I knew she was*
> *buried there – I didn't know where and for months on end I searched*
> *around. And then every day I used to go at break times and say a few*
> *prayers at her grave. It was like a private thing – I had to do it in*
> *secret.*

Louise was relentless in her efforts to establish a 'connection' with her mother. When it was finally made, the connection was maintained against all odds. In a life of adversity, her determination was striking.

We need to pause here and consider the plight of a young bereaved daughter who is terrified that her elders will find out that she sought out her mother's grave and was visiting it on a regular basis. For some, plucking up the courage to ask pertinent questions took time. It was twenty-three years before Maude, whose mother died in childbirth when Maude was seven, knew what had happened to her:

> *I was about thirty and I asked someone what happened my mother*
> *and then they told me.*

Others, such as Lesley, learned about the nature and cause of their mother's death by consulting books. Lesley didn't know or understand what cancer of the colon was but, like Maude, she talked about her great longing to find out exactly what had happened. Eventually, an opportunity to discover more presented itself in the school library. Lesley discovered a book on cancer that enabled her to find information and statistics. She felt 'relieved' that she knew more:

> *The more knowledge you have, the more power you have and the more*
> *understanding you have. The difficulty was, I didn't have any*
> *understanding.*

THE NEED TO CREATE 'A PICTURE'

Helen began digging by contacting the church where her parents were married. She was delighted when the rector was able to release a picture of the wedding that was stored in the archives. Helen said:

> That was the first photograph I had ever seen of her. Although it was black and white ... it was lovely.

Through the information she received, Helen shared with pride how she became aware that it was a big wedding in the late 1950s, with a 'big choral procession and girl guide guard of honour'.

Some time later, Helen also learned where her mother was buried, thanks to her husband who inadvertently found out at another family funeral. After years of waiting to discover its location, she said it was helpful to know where the grave was. It gave her the chance to make her first visit, which she did with her husband.

It was through a few brief conversations with her uncle and aunt that Eleana learned some tiny bits of information about her mother. When she was told that her mother went out on a fishing boat a few times, she understood where and when this took place, so she was able to create an image in her mind's eye. However, as she unveiled this part of her history in the interview, Elena's slow wistful tone conveyed how she valued what little she knew, but also that she wished she knew more.

Over the years, Helen E and Maggie had gleaned some insights that they were delighted to share. Their mothers' lives and personalities took shape and meaning as more became known. Helen E explained:

> People have filled me in on the type of person she was, especially her friend. She told me that she was a scream, she was so funny. She was always doing crazy things like dyeing her hair or putting on fake tan and this sort of thing. She was just the life and soul of the party.

For Maggie, whose mother died when she was five months old, the craving to know more was fulfilled by 'the strong network of women around her' as she grew up. Maggie found out that her mother 'loved children', that she loved 'having an awful lot of people around her'. Most of all her mother 'was very feisty, she was up for a laugh and she was great fun'.

The rich nuggets of information provided psychological nourishment to daughters. No matter how small they brought comfort. It was the joy of finally getting to 'know' their mother that helped. It was the satisfaction of knowing more about the mother who gave birth to them, who brought them into this world, who shared their life for a period of weeks, months or years. She was the person they felt they had a 'right' to know about. But when the facts become known, they had to be digested and coped with (mentally and emotionally). As daughters discovered, the choice to 'dig' had consequences; when the search began and knowledge of their mothers was unearthed in different ways, there were new bits of information to digest and many emotions that accompanied the process.

MIXED BLESSINGS

Every possible piece of evidence that could have helped to create meaning was valued. Regardless of how little or how much information could be gleaned, daughters were thankful for them. And while they had a deep desire to know more about their mothers, they were unprepared for the impact of new knowledge. For example, when she was five years old, Ann's mother died in childbirth. In later years, when she asked her aunt and her cousin about her mother, Ann was initially delighted to hear that her mother was 'so pleasant, so jolly and very outgoing'. But when she was told of her mother's medical history, Ann was presented with the realisation that, had things been dealt with differently, her mother's life might have been saved, and she was left to ponder the possibility that the death could have been prevented if the doctor's advice had been listened to:

> She had put on a lot of weight. She was a very big woman and I think she had been advised not to have any more children. That was always

there – if she hadn't had another baby she wouldn't have died. I think that's maybe why it was very traumatic – she was told not to have more children.

Like Ann and others, Karen learned intimate details about her mother through the family network. She discovered the exact day and month that her mother first felt pain, and the day on which she died. She also knew that the cancer had started in her mother's stomach and that it spread very quickly. The medics made an attempt to operate but to no avail.

Notably, taking part in the interview was *the first time* Karen had spoken about the death and its impact on her. Twenty-six years had elapsed since her mother's death. The opportunity to share her experience was a chance to break the silence. As she unveiled details of the death and loss of her mother and the history that surrounded it, it was as if Karen was sharing a secret. She spoke in soft, whispering tones as the different aspects of her story were gently released for the first time. Perhaps, when people have lived in silence for a long number of years, opening up for the first time can be a struggle. In speaking about the unspoken, people may feel as if they are betraying others, talking about something that has been forbidden, censored and silenced.

Mary B found out that it is not possible to be unaffected by information when it eventually unfolds. When she reached the age her mother was when she died, she was filled with empathy for the plight that her mother had to face:

I came to twenty-nine and I realised what it must have been like for my mother. For seven years she must have known that she wouldn't see us grow up and that must have been difficult.

Mary B outlined the question she was left with:

What was in my mother's mind when she knew that her life was coming to an end and that she would not live to see her children growing up?

While it might be imaginable that daughters would have some difficulty in emotionally processing information that came to light, it was nevertheless important that they learned the truth about their mother. As Patricia said, children need to know, and to grieve properly they need to know the truth.

ACCIDENTAL DISCOVERIES, HYPNOSIS AND OTHER THINGS: UNCOVERING THE EVIDENCE

The teenage years and beyond seemed to increase the strength and potency of the longing to know more. Perhaps as noted by Louise, daughters were at the stage where they recognised that they had a 'right' to information. She was so desperate to know more about her mother that, at the age of fifteen, she decided to see if hypnosis was the answer:

> I did go to a hypnotist when I was about fifteen. I had this thing of wanting to know about her. He was trying to get me to regress to see if I could remember anything.

In the end, hypnosis proved to be a fruitless venture for Louise and 'that was the end of that'.

It took time for daughters to realise the resources or possibilities open to them in terms of finding out about their mothers. In their purposeful, deliberate or 'accidental' attempts to break through the silence, the images of young daughters in search of knowledge were very poignant.

Lesley got tired of waiting to find out how her mother had died and in the end she had to take action:

> I sneaked into my dad's room and I went through documents and found her death certificate.

At that point, she would have learned that it was cancer that brought her mother's life to an end. Like other daughters, in that moment (without prior warning or support), Lesley was confronted with knowledge that was completely new to her.

Like Lesley, Joanna unearthed the death certificate that confirmed miscarriage as the cause of her mother's death. She explained the situation:

> The only reason I found out what actually happened to her is that I came across the death certificate. It was a couple of years before I moved away from home so I must have been about seventeen or eighteen. They just didn't talk about the whole episode.

If we pause for a moment and try to put ourselves in the shoes of young bereaved daughters, we might wonder, for example, in those first moments of gaining new knowledge about their mothers, how did they feel? How were the insights processed mentally and emotionally? What kinds of mental images might they have had? It might be imaginable that there would have been more to think about, more to absorb and more to digest and that such a process would be ongoing, possibly lifelong.

THE NEED TO ASK SOMEBODY BUT NOT KNOWING WHO TO TURN TO

Daughters, starved of information for a long time, know that going through life with little knowledge can be frustrating and emotionally upsetting. They have lived with the uncertainty of approaching family members in case of upsetting them. The reluctance to ask may also have stemmed from the assumption that when people are older 'they would not want to talk'. This was Joanna's dilemma. She wasn't sure that, if she asked her aunt, who was one of the few that might know about her mother, she would be willing to talk. Like others, the fear of causing upset dissuaded her from asking.

But being left in the dark and unable to ask can lead to more stress and emotional upset. Lesley poignantly told how she needed someone to explain things to her and how 'not knowing' impacted on her:

> *I went through periods where I was just very tearful, upset or very*
> *down, and at one stage I thought, I need somebody; I need to ask*
> *somebody and I didn't know who to turn to. I needed to know what*
> *had happened – this was very difficult.*

Not knowing who to turn to for information was a dilemma for the
early bereaved. But it was more exasperating to discover that others
knew things that daughters felt they should have known.

'OTHERS KNEW MORE'

When the roots of knowledge came to light after many years, there
was a rage and anger that erupted. Having been deprived of their
mother's biography for many years, daughters became incensed
when they realised that others (even strangers) knew more about
her than they did. In daughters' minds, it did not make sense that
they, her children, knew little about their mothers while others
were in possession of important information. On this issue,
daughters communicated their frustration and anger in a candid
and forthright manner. Anne stated:

> *It was a very difficult thing for her to be gone and for nobody to talk*
> *about it and then to run in to people who'd say, 'Oh your mother was*
> *a great woman'. Now you tell me these things; when you should have*
> *told me these things, you didn't.*

The more information divulged in this scenario, the angrier
daughters, like Lesley, became:

> *It angers me that there's a stranger I can meet on the street or*
> *someone I could meet through work who knows more about what my*
> *mother was like or what her death was like than I do. I was one of the*
> *youngest of a set of cousins and they all know more than me, and that*
> *angers me.*

Lesley and Anne's messages were directed not only at people they
might have met by chance, but at the family network – the keepers
or holders of information. Lesley raised another important issue

when she aired her fears about losing the 'sources' of information that could provide her with vital information that she felt she needed to begin the process of 'dealing' with the loss:

> I suppose my worst fear would be that I wouldn't deal with it over the next ten years and that maybe people would die and it's too late. What would happen then, because I'll never find out and surely I have that right?

The important questions to be flagged here are, what kind of impact might it have on daughters if the opportunity to learn about their mother is lost? How might a daughter reinforce a 'connection' with her mother if she knows little about her? How might a bereaved daughter build a picture of their mother if no-one is going to help her to do so?

Being in a kind of 'information limbo' was difficult, but conversely, finding out was underpinned by uncertainty. Accessing knowledge was an unknown entity and the thought of it stirred up complex feelings and emotions that then had to be managed. Maggie made the profound observation that the loss of a mother 'shapes and informs how bereaved daughters interact with the world and that they do need to find a place to talk about it'. But while some daughters knew people they could talk to and access information, some were ambivalent about doing so.

KNOWING HOW TO FIND OUT BUT BEING AFRAID TO DO SO

Dara had always 'craved' finding out about her mother. As noted above, there were opportunities to do so when her cousins shared what they knew, usually at family parties. This scenario suited Dara because she felt 'safe' in the situation where others were present – she could contain or 'really control' her emotions. When she was surrounded with people she would not let herself fall apart. But a challenge arose when she discovered that her mother's best friend was back living in her locality after many years of living abroad. The lady extended an invitation to Dara to come to her house to sit down and talk about her mother. So far the visit had been resisted but it was fear and trepidation that kept Dara away. She did try to make the visit happen but it was cut short: 'I went up to her house once but I walked away again.' In those few words, Dara captured the essence of some daughters' feelings about the information-gathering process. It was a process filled with fear of being overwhelmed, of not knowing how to cope with the details of a mother's life as they were revealed. There was uncertainty about the feelings that might erupt and how they might be managed (especially in front of someone). Helen said it was almost as if you had to 'gear yourself up' to access information. This might help to explain daughters' tendencies to avoid rather than confront, and why in some instances they chose to search in secret. Even though there was little in the way of psychological preparation, at least they were alone when the information was unveiled (as when discovering the death certificate), which from a daughters' perspective may be a 'safer' way to learn about their mothers. Perhaps having been excluded from information for so long meant that fear had built up internally and the thought of being close to finding out pushed anxiety levels almost off the scale.

INFORMATION OVERLOAD

When it arose, the opportunity to spend time with the holders of prime knowledge was welcomed. But having to digest and cope with all that might be uncovered in a short space of time was an arduous task. Helen got a shock when she realised there was a discrepancy in the facts as she knew them. From the bits of information gleaned over the years, she was under the impression that she was two-and-a-half when her mother died. However, her mother's death certificate revealed the truth and it came as a surprise:

> When the death certificate came and it said three and a half, it was such a shock. You think, well, that was a year longer than we had realised.

In that profound moment, Helen realised that her mother had been part of her life for a year longer than she had previously thought. Having eventually found the courage to talk to her father, Helen found out about her mother's personality and her parents' relationship, something that she described as definitely helpful. As the picture began to build, a further invitation was accepted. She was invited to visit a member of the choir in which her mother had sang. But Helen revealed that she was ill-prepared for the emotional impact of a long discussion:

> I arrived there at 7.30 p.m. and I was still there at one o'clock in the morning. We talked constantly, and I got an awful lot of information in one night. It really knocked my system for six; I had to take a few days off. It was really quite traumatic.

Information overload had played havoc with her emotions, and her husband supportively suggested that she was going through her grief. Daughters had not bargained for the unexpected outcomes of information seeking. For example, one of the longer-term repercussions of early loss was the need to undergo health checks on a periodic basis, a direct result of their mothers' illness.

INFORMATION RESULTING IN GENETIC/HEALTH SCREENING

Some daughters discovered that regular health checks had to become part of their lives. This was particularly true for those whose mothers died of cancer. In this respect, daughters hoped that sharing detailed descriptions of their experiences would help to enlighten others so that sensitivity might be employed for others in the future.

Lesley was angry at the way in which a screening programme was managed (by both the family and the medical profession). She expressed her anger at not being properly informed by her father or the doctor about the tests that she was about to endure at the time. She described her experience and was anxious that others would be advised by her detailed account:

Unknown to me, we had to go to our doctor and my brother and myself had to get blood tests. We didn't really know what they were. What was your colon? What were the risks? What were the tests? It was only really after the tests that I found out what a sigmoidoscopy was. I remember going to my appointment. It was in my teenage years and my father had taken me to the hospital – he wasn't invited to come in with me. The doctor said, 'Your mother died, is that right?' I knew it was something to do with cancer, and my grandmother had breast cancer as well. I didn't know what the difference between one kind of cancer and another was. He asked me to get up on the table and he performed the test and I remember being horrified. Obviously at that age I didn't know what was going on. He didn't explain very well what he was doing. He said, 'I am going to insert this camera and it might be painful'.

I came out and I cried all the way home on the bus. My father couldn't understand and he said, 'Are you ok?' I said, 'How would you feel if somebody shoved a camera inside of you?' I was angry because he didn't explain what was going to happen. He just wasn't aware, and I found out later that the same thing happened my brother and he was obviously horrified. He was younger than me and I suppose there was a lot of anger there. I can see that my father is so caring but he doesn't have the ability to pass on or express anything about my mother.

Being screened became compulsory when the first signs of bowel cancer (that had caused their mother's death) was discovered in Louise's family. They are all currently on a screening programme.

The doctors decided to examine the whole family, boys and girls. It was only last summer and we were all taken in and had to have tests done, and for the rest of our lives we have to have these tests done every five years – colonoscopies.

While there was some level of acceptance that tests 'had to be done', the process was not an inclusive one and there was a lack of sensitivity shown by all concerned. Being kept in the dark about the nature of the tests resonated with the silence that had dominated daughters' lives. These accounts raised awareness of the need for careful management in carrying out health checks, particularly with those who have suffered significant loss and who may feel especially vulnerable during such events.

NOT DIGGING

The preference not to 'dig' was partly due to consideration for the feelings of other family members. But some daughters also held the view that, having survived for years without information, there were other ways of managing. Elizabeth summarised:

> We have survived this long – now you would rather just not dig, just think about her from time to time.

The fears and concerns expressed by daughters in the study were endorsed by the maternally bereaved who attended the presentation of the study in London (July 2005). Some affirmed the 'very real' fear associated with finding out about mothers and coping with the knowledge and information gained. However, as noted by a member of the audience, 'You have to deal with it some day', inferring that the bereaved cannot run forever from their loss and that to deal with the death and its impact, the truth and facts were important. Another member of the audience very wisely added that much depended upon the way in which and by whom a mother's history was relayed to her children.

Daughters in the study who wished to break the silence had to persist. They had to find strength and resources to unearth the knowledge and information they needed. The 'need to know' that engulfed them was very simply and succinctly expressed by Lesley in the words: 'I needed to know what had happened.'

At the time of the interviews, the search for knowledge and information was ongoing. Without the necessary changes, the search for knowledge will remain an eternal one. However, on a positive note, Anne thought that times have now changed and that: 'People are more aware of children's feelings and possibly people find it easier to talk about death.'

4. 'MILESTONES IN YOUR LIFE'

I remember the first time it hit me was probably when I was getting married and I couldn't believe how much of an impact it had that I didn't have a mother; the birth of children, important things like that, you know, milestones in your life – Helen E.

The adventures that are part of play in the childhood of daughters throughout the world – dressing up as a bride, pretending to be a mammy – are sometimes played out for real in later life. In general, occasions such as a wedding day or the birth of a baby are regarded as events to be cherished and celebrated. Similarly, the annual celebration of motherhood, Mother's Day, is widely embraced in society. For the early bereaved, however, significant life events are marked by the fact that their mother is not there to share the experience with them. While there can be offers of help and support around at the time, daughters realise that they will not undergo transitional events in the same way that others do. Their experiences are marked and coloured by the fact that they are without their mother; the shadow that is cast over their lives by her absence is particularly acute on days that are special. As Pauline stated: 'Things will trigger it off throughout your life, like the first baby being born and getting married.'

RENEWED LOSS

Daughters were unprepared for the ways in which the loss impacted on them as they approached important events. A renewed sense of loss can come almost like a 'bolt out of the blue'; it can 'hit very hard'. The shock-like reaction that daughters experience can occur for a few reasons. At the time of the death and in the years following, the pain of the loss may be so hard to bear that it becomes deeply repressed – it is, as it were, put out of reach. Throughout the years, there may be little opportunity to begin the process of mourning or grieving the loss. In the early years, living in a climate of silence and lack of emotional support creates little space for grieving to begin. As a result, daughters learn to bottle up their thoughts and feelings, the multitude of worries and concerns they carry concealed from those around them. Given these conditions, there may be little chance for contemplation or discussion of the implications of the loss with adults. According to the daughters who shared their experiences, the lack of talking meant that they were vastly unprepared for the way in which the loss might impact on them as they approached important milestones. Therefore, when it came to significant events like getting married, being pregnant or becoming a mother, they were 'hit' with a renewed sense of loss and grief. Once triggered, it is acutely felt.

One of the most difficult aspects in the run up to special occasions is coping with the mixture of feelings and emotions that are stirred as the loss resurfaces. Facing major life hurdles as an early bereaved daughter changes the nature of the event, how it is perceived and how it is experienced – all of which may be invisible to others. It is a time that exacerbates that deep sense of loss. A mother's presence is 'missed' and the 'gap' cannot be filled.

'IT HIT ME WHEN I WAS GETTING MARRIED'

Helen E recalls what it was like when she got married at twenty-one:

> I was nine when she died, so the first time it hit me was when I was getting married, and it hit me very hard.

What could be a memorable and exciting time is clouded by unhappiness and upset, of which others may not be aware.

Pauline said that the loss of her mother had such a grip at the time that it was 'horrendous getting married'. However, her wedding day was brightened with a surprise. She decided to get married when she was seventeen – a move her husband-to-be claimed was her endeavour to 'get out of the house'. On the day of the wedding, Pauline's cousin arrived at her house early in the morning and said, 'I have something for you – put out your hand'. To her delight and surprise, Pauline was presented with her mother's eternity ring, a significant gesture on such an important day. It not only cheered her up but, as Pauline explained, it also helped to alleviate her disappointment and annoyance that nothing was bequeathed to her following the death of her mother. At seventeen, however, she discovered that adjusting to marriage and making it work was extremely difficult. Pauline admitted that, at the start, things were really tough when they were getting used to living with one another. It took a while to settle into married life!

As a way of coping, Alison made a decision similar to Pauline's. She said that she wanted to invest in a new life and to recreate what was lost. In her search for a new role and identity, and spurred on by a feeling of having 'lost out' and 'craving for love', Alison sadly found herself in a marriage that was 'doomed from the beginning':

> I look back and think, why did I get married, because I suppose from the start I knew myself it wasn't going to work. Looking back now he wasn't marriage material – he was very selfish and all the rest. I suppose I just wanted my own family unit and my own place. I just wanted someone that was there for me because I felt that I had lost out. I was craving for love for me so I went into this marriage and it lasted four years and eventually he left. At the time I was devastated, but I soon picked myself up and got on with it. I suppose losing my mother and having such regimented teenage years, I have been able to stand on my own two feet; when my mother died I had to grow up very, very quickly.

Even though there may be offers of help and support, every step of the way is marked by a mother's absence. A sense of unfairness and frustration is echoed in Helen E's reflection:

> Daughters always have their mothers around them and I don't have mine and I'm upset.

Karen, who was nine when her mother died, poignantly recalls a moment in the lead-up to her wedding when it was time to try on her dress:

> One of my brothers came to see me in my wedding dress at the shop. It was sad with her not being there; you know that there is going to be no-one to fill that place.

In thinking about finding someone to 'fill that place', thirty-four-year-old Pauline pondered over the question, who would you ask to stand in for your mother? She discovered that trying to select someone to step into her mother's shoes was not easy, especially with so many aunties who were all willing to help and contribute at the time of the wedding. The trick then is how to choose one without offending the rest. A bereaved daughter knows how difficult it is to cope and get into the spirit of it all. She may choose not to voice or share her inner feelings in case of upsetting others or becoming upset in front of family members, a pattern learned in early life.

Ann recalls how the death of her father just before her wedding was a significant blow. One of the greatest fears for children is that the surviving parent may die. When the loss occurs in adulthood it is felt just as strongly. The important person to whom she became deeply attached and who had remained in her life for a long number of years is not there to carry out the traditional custom of giving his daughter away. The timing of his death and the 'complete parenting role' that he had fulfilled meant that his absence was deeply felt at the time. 'There was a great gap with him not there,' Ann explains. A father who is highly regarded and who plays a significant role in the aftermath of a mother's death will be sorely missed on such an important day.

The importance of reaching a level of acceptance before the wedding day was raised by Anne. She discovered a ritual that helped her survive the hurdle of getting married, one that she strongly recommends to others. The suggestion is that prior to their wedding, maternally bereaved daughters should visit their mother's grave (with family members for support) to mourn and grieve the fact that their mother is not going to be part of the special day. Taking the time to let feelings out in this way may have a settling effect on emotions. Having honoured their mother's memory and the fact that she will be absent may help daughters to get through the day.

The turmoil of having to cope with other wedding related anxieties can bring additional stress to bear. Joanna's registry office wedding was not well received by her stepmother, who exclaimed, 'It's not a real wedding'. She found this comment to be hurtful. Similarly, Helen was baffled and perplexed by her stepmother's insistence that her status within the family was not left open to question at the wedding:

> I remember when I was getting married my stepmother said: 'I don't want any reference at this wedding to the fact that I'm not your mother'.

Unhelpful comments that hurt and confuse cause regret, particularly since the most important aspect of the day for daughters is that their natural mother's memory is honoured as part of the ceremony.

The feelings that daughters experience during pregnancy are similar to those that they encounter getting married. Pregnancy is not a normal life transition for the early bereaved, as it might be for others. It too is a time when a mother is sorely missed and the feelings of loneliness that daughters experience are often there because their self-esteem has suffered and there has been little chance to mourn the death and loss of their mother. Expecting a baby in the absence of a mother brings many feelings to the fore.

'MISSING OUT DURING PREGNANCY – THAT WOULD HAVE BEEN THE WORST TIME'

Dara describes how the feelings of loss was reactivated during her pregnancies:

> When I got pregnant it was really bad because I really, really wanted her; that would have been the worst time.

The sense of yearning in these heartfelt words affirmed that a bereaved daughter in her months of pregnancy and on the brink of becoming a mother herself (for the first, second or whatever time) feels the sense of loss acutely. It is one of those times in life when a mother can be the one to share the news with, to confide in and seek advice, to even compare notes! But the opportunity to do so is denied. Others may willingly offer help and it will be appreciated, but nothing will prevent daughters from longing for the presence of a mother. There may be people to turn to for help and support, but regardless of how good they are, it is a 'different relationship', as Clare thought, and it doesn't mean that daughters will escape the feelings of loss inside of them.

It was the sense of low self-esteem and loneliness with which Kathleen grew up that took its toll when she became pregnant in her early twenties. Throughout her pregnancy she felt unable to confide in anyone. It was a very lonely period of her life:

> I would have loved to have had a mother to confide in and to talk to. I didn't tell one person that I was pregnant.

In her search for love and affection, a pregnancy occurred, but her loss and its repercussions created such fear and uncertainty that it was not possible to trust or reach out to anyone, even those closest. Entering motherhood is one of the most difficult transitional periods for daughters who are without their mother. It is a time when further realisations hit and doubts and uncertainties arise. Almost inevitably, a new cycle of mourning is reactivated.

'THE BIRTH OF MY CHILDREN ... IT HIT ME THEN'

When a baby arrived and a new phase of life began, daughters were overwhelmed with the depth and breadth of feelings they experienced at the time and in the months and years ahead. Helen E and Mary recalled how it can hit harder with the first baby:

> The birth of my children, it hit me then; when I had the first child, that was when I missed her a lot.

Mothers are not there to share the event or offer motherly support to daughters as they cope with the new role. There is the realisation that she will never know the child or subsequent children and that they will never know her. For Elizabeth, the fact that neither parent was alive to witness the birth of her children brought sadness and a hope that history would not repeat itself. She was ten when her mother died and in her early twenties when her children were born. Elizabeth explains how she felt:

> I found that it was a sad time them being born and none of my parents around to see them. I've always said to our children that I would love to see my grandchildren. I wouldn't like the same thing to happen to them because I found that a missing time.

Daughters know what it means to lose a mother in early life; they know the impact of the loss at the time and in the years ahead. When they enter motherhood, daughters also know what it means to not have a mother to turn to or share the event with. This is something they hope their own children will escape and this is a worry they live with. Some said it was also the loss of a role model to observe and imitate as they embraced their new role in life that they mourned.

'I HAD NO IDEA OF MOTHERING SKILLS, AND BABIES DON'T COME WITH AN INSTRUCTION MANUAL'

Motherhood is a time when countless feelings and emotions erupt as a consequence of the loss – missing, yearning, annoyance, questions and much more. It's not surprising then that daughters associate difficulties in parenting with the loss of a role model. Not only that, while daughters attempt to parent their own children, they also crave to be parented. There is a deep desire to be cared for, nurtured, supported and guided. The craving for what is missing is so powerful that it can overshadow and threaten the ability to parent a child. In a sense, the arrival of the newborn baby and the beginning of motherhood is bittersweet. Becoming a mother can be gratifying because the baby is a new life to focus on and cherish. At the same time, the heightened sense of loss triggers a cycle of grief and mourning. There is a range of complex feelings that are all happening at once: happiness accompanies sadness; joy is overshadowed by yearning.

As daughters embark on their new role in life, the lack of their own mother's presence brings feelings and emotions to the surface. There is a sense of aloneness, 'not having somebody there to help you through it'. Maureen outlined her confusion about how to be a mother and the importance of having a mother to show her the ropes:

> I had no idea of mothering skills, and babies don't come with an instruction manual. I hadn't a notion – talk about being thrown in at the deep end! You pick up a lot of things from your mother. I can notice it now when watching mothers and their children, things that I didn't know and skills that are probably handed down.

Mary appreciated the help she received when her children were born but the deeply felt loss of her mother remained:

> I remember my mother-in-law was very good to me and that made a big difference. But I always felt the loss, especially in the years between the time I got married and the children growing up.

The lack of a role model left daughters questioning their own ability to be a good mother. As Joanna exasperatedly said:

> How the hell am I supposed to do this right when I haven't had anybody to show me?

She was living away from the extended family when her children were born and being in another country at the time meant that she had no-one to turn to – hence she lost out on 'wee hints on how to cope with things' that other family members might have been able to offer her.

As a mother, Karen loves her children but she found it difficult to offer them what she had lost out on in her own childhood:

> I should be more chilled out and relaxed. I'm good to them, I love them and they love me. I definitely think that what you get at home is what makes you a good parent. I should make more time to sit and nurse them. I'm always busy. I just feel – should I be a better parent?

But not everyone agrees that a role model is necessary. Patricia's philosophy is that 'motherhood is a natural thing, there are no role models needed for you to be a good parent'. Others felt that older sisters can sometimes take up the mantle of role model. However, it was agreed that once the role is set in place, the responsibility can remain indefinitely. Once Elizabeth's sister became 'a role model replacing her mother', she remained the one that everyone went to when there was a problem. In essence, it becames a job for life! Dara agrees, because herself and her brother became the surrogate 'Mammy and Daddy' in the family. To this day they remain the problem solvers and the advice givers.

'I MISSED NOT BEING ABLE TO GO OUT AND BUY A MOTHER'S DAY CARD'

Growing up, daughters have to learn to cope with the annual milestone of Mother's Day. Earlier, Lesley helped us to understand how the task of making a Mother's Day card in school can be a 'nightmare' for an early bereaved child. It has to be remembered that it is a day that daughters cannot participate in. As others celebrate the significance of the event, maternally bereaved daughters endure it rather than celebrate it. The day casts its own shadow over daughters' lives, making the loss more pronounced. Buying a card is one of the tasks that symbolises the industry that Mother's Day has become, but as Maureen also suggested, this makes bereaved daughters more acutely aware of the day and its meaning. Daughters know the kind of endurance test the day is: 'I miss not being able to go out and buy a Mother's Day card.' A wish simply expressed but with far-reaching implications. Others were faced with the challenge of buying a card when instructed to do so. Thirty-five year old Joanna, whose mother died when she was three, explains:

> Mother's Day is so difficult. When you are buying the card, what on earth do you do? What kind of card do you get for a stepmother? I didn't want to buy her one, but my dad made it clear that we had to. You read all the little verses and then on the front they have 'Mum' on them. I would try to find a card that would be as correct as possible without being gushy and all that sort of thing.

These words evoke images of a daughter's struggle to honour her own wishes while honouring her father's wishes. The task of choosing a Mother's Day card may be a source of joy and pleasure for many but there is a need for sensitivity around those who experience it differently. One daughter, Liz, whose mother died when she was five months old, recalls the resentment and anger she felt when other daughters were buying Mother's Day cards and presents. Their insensitivity to the fact that her mother had died was unwelcome:

> I remember at a point in my life becoming aware of this thing called Mother's Day and that girls were buying Mother's Day cards and presents and things like that. Of course the girls, and I understand that it was a slip of the tongue, they would say, 'What are you buying for your mummy?' And I said 'I have no mummy, I don't have to buy

anything, I never had a mummy'. I think that brought an element of resentment out as well. I can clearly remember that I felt angry – you know, don't bother me with this Mother's Day nonsense, it doesn't apply to me.

If your mother died when you were young, being confronted with the question, 'What are you buying for your mummy?' can cause embarrassment, humiliation and resentment. In that moment coping is difficult, and a self-defensive reaction may be the only form of self-protection.

On Mother's Day (Mothering Sunday), bereaved daughters have their own rituals or ways of honouring the memory of their mothers. For some, visiting the grave may be a long-standing custom; however, the passage of time does not make it any easier. Supportive partners can play a significant role in helping the early bereaved. Having someone who shows understanding and offers help and support when needed can make a difference. But it takes foresight and thought on the part of those involved to ensure that support is in place. Without the help of a partner who was 'in tune with things', Dara would have resisted the visit:

I was avoiding it, I was doing that cut-off thing – I'm not going there, I'm not doing it.

This was another form of self-protection. However, the situation was managed when Dara was taken to the cemetery because her partner recognised that she needed to be there. Not only that, he had a bunch of flowers in the boot of the car and gave them to her to put on her mother's grave. This was appreciated.

Fathers too can be sensitive to their daughter's struggle. Helen began Mother's Day one year in very poor form. She was 'feeling so rotten' that she didn't want to go to the cemetery. Part of the normal routine was to get flowers and go with her father to put them on the grave. However, a timely and comforting phone call from her father saved the day and they went together to honour her mother's memory. What helps is sensitivity and input from other people. Sometimes, a grieving daughter needs help and encouragement to face the situation that she very badly wants to partake in, but is avoiding.

Daughters gradually discover the legacy of the loss as life unfolds. Around special occasions in particular it can 'hit very hard'. It's when the realisation hits that the daughters will not know the meaning of what it is to share their wedding, pregnancy, the birth of their children, motherhood or Mother's Day with a mother that they suffer. As this sinks in, the grief can be fresh and raw, overwhelming. On top of the stress that is normally associated with significant occasions, such as a wedding, pregnancy or the birth of a baby, bereaved daughters have the psychological 'weight' of the loss to bear. The yearning for what is lost – the role model, the nurturer, the mother who instructs, guides and supports – is reawakened.

We need to be mindful that whether or not a daughter remembers her mother, the loss of her will be felt continually throughout life. If a mother died in the very early weeks, months or years of her daughter's life, that daughter will forever know her life is different because her mother is not present.

5. 'YOU LEARN TO COVER YOUR HEART'

I hate to get in too close and lose somebody again. I would hold back, I wouldn't want to go through that again. There's not too many would get in really deep; I think it's just that you learn to cover your heart – Theresa.

We know and appreciate that children have a basic need to be cared for and looked after by someone. When they need attention, affection or support, children look to the person they rely on most to attend to their needs. There is usually one person who is the main carer, and it is a role mostly fulfilled by the child's mother. Traditionally, the mother is regarded as the heart of the family, the central source of learning and support, the primary nurturer, carer and teacher. However, when it is the case that children are permanently separated from their mother due to her untimely death, everything changes. It cannot be guaranteed that the need a youngster has for love, trust and support will be met. It is understandable that when any sense of security and stability that existed in family life is undone through death, the journey ahead for everyone concerned will be different. Now that trust is broken, how is the child going to trust again? Who is going to meet the needs of the child now? These are the worries that bereaved children carry with them.

When trust is shattered in early life, the emotional fallout can be immeasurable. As early bereaved daughters discovered, the loss of their mother and the many consequences that ensued in the years after took a toll on their mental, emotional and physical health. Many felt, as Lesley did, that it was the death and all the 'spin-offs' that wreaked havoc with their psychological health. Then others, like Helen and Liz, attributed their loss of self-esteem or loss of confidence more to the repercussions that followed the loss of their mother, rather than the fact that she died. This was partly the case because the death of their mother occurred when they were very young – at the age of three-and-a-half and five months respectively. Therefore, it was not knowing her and not having a memory of their mother that led them to conclude that her death had less of an impact.

Despite their emotional difficulties, daughters (as many children do) found ways of coping with the legacy they inherited through death (as this chapter will reveal).

THE BURDEN OF THE LOSS

It was never going to be easy for youngsters starting off in life with an emotional struggle brought about by unexpected or unforeseen circumstances. The loss put at risk their chances of having positive experiences that could have potentially boosted their self-esteem and confidence. This was, in short, what daughters discovered – that a strong sense of self-worth and self-esteem evaded them. Life for them was not as it should have been. It was a life that took on a different tone and meaning, as Maggie succinctly summarised: 'You come through life with this huge burden on your shoulders.'

What we need to remember is that daughters had grown up with the experience of loss. They knew what it was, what it is, to lose. These women, now adults, had survived the death of their mother in their early life and the consequences that ensued. It was a unique and not so common heritage and, therefore, maybe not a phenomenon that was well understood. Sometimes, people don't 'see' the burden that children and adult survivors carry inside. Throughout life, the burden can remain 'unseen', nevertheless it has implications for an individual's self-esteem, confidence and sense of security; it impacts on relationships in life including those with other people and partners, with fathers and with children; and a multitude of fears and emotions erupt over the lifespan, which lead to illness, anxiety and depression.

'I FELT ABANDONED – WE ALL FELT ABANDONED'

Daughters who were old enough to remember their mothers had a sense of being emotionally deserted or abandoned. Anne lamented: 'I felt abandoned, I think we all felt abandoned.' It was not only the permanent separation from their mother that they were referring to, it was a sense of being abandoned by the adults around them who were struggling to cope with their own feelings in the aftermath of the loss. Grieving adults may have little to offer young bereaved children but it might be imaginable that they worry about their inability to aid the young through grief and loss.

Dara said that the 'hang ups' she experienced continually throughout life were down to her mother dying and the life she had after that. Despite efforts on the part of others to inject support and help into their lives, such as aunts or cousins visiting regularly, daughters had a residue of feelings that were 'bottled up' inside.

'THE LOSS SHAPES YOU EMOTIONALLY'

It was the loss of the opportunity for love and affection, the sense of abandonment, the unhappiness, loneliness and sense of isolation that swamped daughters. In the aftermath, they developed a neediness that became almost unappeasable. Enough was never enough. People might have tried to help but what daughters really wanted was their mother; all other efforts, while welcomed, could not replace their deep desire for her. Ultimately, the loss helped to form daughters' emotional outlooks, as Maggie explained:

> That loss cannot be filled. It's a bottomless pit, that emotional loss is – you want so much from other people.

The lack of an emotional support system meant that daughters had to almost exist alone emotionally. There were those like Louise who suggested that because there was 'absolutely no love' at the time, she realised that even as a child in school she was 'craving love'. It was the very, very lonely feeling and sense of terrible isolation from the age of five or six that Louise found the hardest to cope with. Kathleen too spoke of having a lonely existence and of not being happy from the death of her mother when she was eleven until she was thirty years old. For Joanna, it was the sense of having 'nobody to turn to' that bothered her most. From her perspective, others would have their mum and dad to turn to when everything goes haywire in life; others would have had back-up and support when it was needed, and she had missed out on that. Abbey said that the lack of love influenced her way of being in the present day:

> I'm quite a touchy feely person, and need to touched, probably because I didn't get that.

For some the dearth of love that existed had a 'hardening' effect on their emotions. Daughters like Liz and Joanna were in agreement that it has made them 'harder' people.

EMOTIONALLY HARDENED

Not being able to talk about their deceased mother or share their concerns with adults compounded daughters' feelings of isolation, loneliness and unhappiness. Some confirmed that being left without their mother had indeed a 'hardening' effect on the emotions. Daughters were not only dealing with the loss but also the lack of opportunity to mourn and grieve her death. Therefore, becoming 'hardened' may have been a coping mechanism. The idea was, toughen up to keep from feeling the feelings or allowing anyone 'in'.

Liz highlighted an important point about her emotional psyche that may well pertain to other early bereaved people. It's a message that we should compassionately note. Like many bereaved daughters, unused to love and support, Liz found that when expressions of concern or sympathy were presented to her, they touched a fragile, vulnerable spot inside that caused her emotions to erupt. During the focus group interaction where five of the daughters met, Liz articulated her feelings:

> I am very, very strong in most ways except for one thing, I can't tolerate kindness; I cry if people are overly sympathetic to me. I can keep fine and strong and not let go of my emotions but if people are kind, are overly sympathetic, that's what will break me.

Others nodded in support as they identified with the experience.

What we can learn from Liz's input is that when kindness, compassion or sympathy are offered, the strong exterior disintegrates. What this reveals is that, at their core, bereaved daughters still feel raw and sensitive, and concern or attention from others touches that vulnerable spot inside of them. Having gained this insight we now know that when we interact with the early bereaved we might consider what it is like to be in their shoes. 'Knowing' alerts all of us to the sensitivity and compassion that is needed around the early bereaved or anyone who has suffered adversity in their lives.

'WE ARE NOT LEFT OUT IN THE WILDERNESS ANYMORE'

Having mentioned the focus group above, there is an important point to be noted here. The day that the daughters met was indeed a poignant occasion for all concerned. It was the first time that daughters had met or spoken with other survivors of early loss outside of their families, and there was a realisation that they had opened a door that was closed for a very long time. Louise captured the sense of what everyone was feeling:

> When I saw your advertisement in the paper, it really hit home with me. I thought, gosh, you know, there really are people who have gone through similar situations. It's just nice to see that there is an interest being taken now. We are not left out in the wilderness anymore.

In essence, by participating in the study daughters had helped themselves to gain a voice, to be heard. Those who were able to attend the focus group at the time confirmed that, difficult as the topic was, there was a need for the study. Their hope was that by sharing their experiences and providing clear messages for the public domain, they would help others and help to validate the early loss of a mother that many have experienced in Ireland and elsewhere.

Through powerful and compelling revelations, daughters provided an insight into the detrimental effects of their experience of loss and the chasm it created in their sense of themselves. Some daughters suffered a double or triple blow: their self-esteem was lowered in the first instance by the loss, secondly by the lack of a shared process of mourning and grieving within their families and thirdly by other negative events that ensued for some throughout life. In sharing their reflections, daughters' stories not only resonated with each other, but they may well resonate with many who are reading this book.

'THE DEATH OF MY MOTHER KNOCKED THE STUFFING OUT OF ME'

Many people cherish the thought of having the high self-esteem or self-worth that is manifested in how they regard and take care of themselves. A person's level of esteem is determined by the foundation created in early life – having needs met, feeling secure, loved and accepted. If we escape deep-seated feelings of insecurity, we might have a chance of cultivating a healthy sense of self as we grow and develop. But if a child experienced or experiences major loss, it has a damaging effect on the self-esteem and their psychological future is permanently shaped by the event.

Having their mothers wrenched out of their lives changed daughters' view of themselves and their view of the world. Any chance of steering a course towards high self-esteem was thwarted; it went completely off course as their self-esteem and confidence levels plummeted. Anne's powerful metaphor captured the depth and intensity that many daughters shared: 'The death of my mother knocked the stuffing out of me.' With such powerful imagery we can imagine a young girl, thriving in life, suddenly being immobilised, as if her lifeblood was removed.

Elaine helped us to understand the depths to which loss can diminish a daughter's self-esteem and confidence. In a heartfelt reflection on childhood, she conveyed how deeply the loss penetrated her psyche. She remembered feeling that it wasn't worth anybody's time taking a photo of her, or that she didn't look particularly good. No-one really knew at the time that this was how Elaine felt. However, we know *now* and that is important. Now that we know that children can suffer in this way we can be more attuned to their internal world.

Theresa was plagued with a fear of speaking and a fear of rejection: 'You were afraid to open your mouth. Are people going to like me or not?' Kathleen had no-one to talk to about how she felt and her self-esteem was so 'shattered' that she wasn't sure if anyone might want to talk to her.

However, for Kathleen and Maureen determination prevailed. They felt that succeeding in their education was a way of salvaging their self-esteem. Kathleen wanted to succeed to honour her mother's wishes that she do well in school. In returning to education, Maureen was driven by another desire:

> It was only really to prove to myself that I wasn't stupid, because my self-esteem was rock bottom.

One of the difficulties was that no matter how much others might have tried to intervene with consistent support, the lack of esteem persisted. Clare explained how the people that she worked with tried to give her self-esteem a boost, but with little success:

> *In the work situation, people have been telling me for years and years,*
> *'You are better than you think; you are better than you think you*
> *come across', and even though they keep telling me this, the insecurity*
> *is still there.*

No matter how well-intentioned others are, when self-esteem and confidence are lowered, recovery does not come about easily. No matter how hard bereaved children or adults try to cover up what lies beneath the surface, others see beyond the exterior and try to help. But covering up and 'protecting' themselves is an important aspect of life for the early bereaved. Daughters did not want to leave themselves open to discussions about their mother or to experience any related feelings, especially when they were around other people. Therefore, finding ways of protecting themselves, such as becoming emotionally hardened, served the purpose well because it was a way of covering up their 'wounds'.

PROTECTIVE ARMOUR

We know that people make judgements when they observe others in various life situations and that impressions sometimes stick. But we need to be mindful that what we have observed, particularly in those who have suffered adversity, may be a brave front, designed indeed to 'cover their hearts'.

This 'armour' can mislead others, as some daughters discovered. For example, people made assumptions about Abbey:

> *Outwardly people say I have a very bubbly personality: I'm always*
> *joking, I'm always laughing, I'm always smiling – no matter what*
> *happens, I'm always smiling. But I think that's my armour,*
> *protecting myself.*

Joanna too recognised that her need to over-compensate through 'loud raucous laughter' when she was out in company was 'all a kind of a front'. She was convinced that no-one really knew that she was covering up how she really felt. Lesley had covering-up down to a fine art:

People think that I am a very confident person, and I'm not. I am very self-conscious.

It was feeling different and feeling insecure that presented daughters with some of their biggest challenges in life. The legacy of insecurity was enduring and in turn created fears and uncertainty. The most important thing was to avoid feeling anything, especially in front of others. When 'warning signs', such as a 'sick feeling in her stomach', indicated to Dara that strong emotions or feelings were about to surface, she took steps to avert the situation. She found it best to go into a neutral mode, a strategy that allowed her to get a 'grip' on the emotions:

When I slip and I fall into my emotions, I catch myself and go straight back as if I'm talking about the woman next door – because I can feel that sick feeling in my stomach and I know then, right, get a grip.

'YOU ARE NOT THE SAME AS EVERYBODY ELSE; YOU CAN'T BE THE SAME AS EVERYBODY ELSE'

Theresa explained that:

Being bereaved early in life means that you are not the same as everybody else and you can't be the same as everybody else.

As noted earlier, sometimes the sense of being 'different' is reinforced in school where other youngsters tease the bereaved. When they are teased, children feel stigmatised for having lost a parent, for being different. The survivors of early loss have a 'big hole' in their lives and because of that they can be very guarded and very insecure, and as Helen said: 'It takes a while to break down barriers.' Living with feelings of insecurity continues to dictate how daughters feel about themselves. Joanna said she 'is always craving reassurance' while Mary lives with self-doubt:

I'm always scared of making a mistake. I'm always scared of offending people or annoying people. I don't like to get on the wrong side of people. Maybe I'm just looking to be liked, wanting everybody to like me.

Searching for reassurance was profoundly difficult given the emotional struggle that everyone was going through. The impact on the emotional health of fathers and daughters had an adverse effect on relationships. Daughters, indeed, learned to cover their hearts, to keep their distance from others, to guard against closeness in relationships.

'YOU LEARN TO COVER YOUR HEART'

When children live with pervasive fear, it impacts on their ability to relate to others because, for them, trusting others and being open is risky. The fear, as aptly illustrated above, is that loss will be repeated so it is better to keep people at arm's length and not risk having to go through the pain again. Maggie says the lack of trust comes from the 'disconnection, abandonment' or the sense of rejection that was experienced at such a young age. To really know how the lack of trust impacted, we turn again to the voices of daughters who explained:

> People have said that I'm emotionally constipated, emotionally autistic, but it's just a protection thing; it is just a way of protecting yourself. My mother died, my mother went and left me, and I'm not going to let anyone else do that. And for a long, long time I was really angry with her. It was only recently that I was able to say that out loud; even though I was thinking it, I was afraid to say it out loud. Now, I would say this isn't bloody fair, you know. But it was definitely the worst thing that ever happened in my life – Dara.

> I don't trust people. People almost need to prove themselves to me. That's something that I'm trying to deal with as I get older. I find sometimes that I'm quite insecure. I am always very wary of people. I don't discuss my past with even some of my closest friends. They've maybe known me for ten years and don't know everything that went on, and I don't talk about it with them. So that's something that I think has affected me: I don't trust easily. If I begin to trust someone

and someone lets me down, no matter how small, I'll be hurt, very, very hurt – Abbey.

I just can't click with people, I just don't. I can't get in with people too close. I would never let my guard down completely with anybody. I'm constantly searching for this best friend that I am never going to find, and with older women in particular I tend to look for their approval, and I don't even know I am doing it. At work my boss is a lady and I would be constantly looking for her approval – Jennifer.

I am very reluctant to let people in. I don't know if it's that I am frightened of losing them – Clare.

I couldn't imagine ever meeting anyone that I could relate to on a level that I could trust; trust has been absent from my life, that is what's wrong with my life. I find it very hard to trust people. I could never let go. I could not put my life in anyone else's hands, I couldn't do it – Liz.

In very powerful and compelling language, daughters provide an insight into their world that leaves us in no doubt that the emotional wound is immensely deep. How could daughters trust again when their world has been so severely rocked and disrupted? How could they trust again when they didn't have a chance to understand what had happened or have help to understand their feelings at the time of their mother's death and beyond? In these conditions, it is almost as if psychological and emotional problems are inevitable. The residue of emotions that remain bottled up inside are driven by the lack of trust and the underlying fear of losing again. It creates within daughters deeply imbedded fears – of death, of rejection, of people. However, in their desperation to cope, a resourceful antidote was revealed.

MENTALLY SELECTING A MOTHER FIGURE

In life people find many ways of coping with the difficulties they face. We all look through a different lens, and therefore the choice a person makes may be very different to that of another. However, we should not be judged for the choices we make, especially if they are helping us to find our way through adversity. Daughters' emotional difficulties were manifest through feelings of anger and hurt and through the need for approval.

Perhaps the need for approval that Jennifer spoke of was motivated by the desire to impress someone who was representative of a mother-type figure, and that it would somehow be gratifying to attain that approval. It was in *mentally* selecting a mother figure that Louise found solace and a sense of feeling safe and secure – a strategy that she talked at length about. She revealed that she was not the only member of her family who employed the strategy. In Louise's case, the person she 'selected' would have shared her mother's physical characteristics (looks, hair, appearance). It turned out to be a fruitful way of bringing a sense of safety and security into her daily existence:

> In my head I would select a teacher, just mentally, and think to myself, she is my mammy. For this year she is looking after me. That is how I coped and I know for a fact that I am not the only one in the family to have done that. Right up until I was about twenty-two, even in [profession] I would have picked a [name of role] and I mightn't have spoken two words to them but in my head this was my mother and this was just a thing to cope, a security. It did help – it was just a thing to make me feel secure, telling myself that I did have a mother.

> I always picked people that I knew were very good and something told me they were nice people. And that is the way I coped through life, and I used to look forward to going to those [name of area] or going to those classes. I used to feel instinctively that I knew a good person by observing them. I would sort of pick out who I thought were the good people and they then became my mother. Even physically as well, there were times there have been people I encountered through my life and I knew they were good people.

From what I was told about my mother, I would have looked at their features and their hair and their physical appearance and I'd go, she's like Mammy, and I'd have liked her instantly [laughs]. I would automatically look for that and just feel some sort of connection. It was a small thing, but it was one good thing that sort of made you feel you could cope a wee bit better. It was like a security thing and I'd feel safe. When it happened I would automatically feel safe.

Louise's story confirms that there were/are means and methods of coping. As each life event happened or was contemplated, thoughts and feelings were influenced by the early loss experience. At this point, we now turn to address one of the areas that daughters shared deep concerns about – the role of motherhood.

THE MOTHERING ROLE

As indicated earlier, reaching the 'milestone' of motherhood was a time when many realisations 'hit'. It was a time when the enormity of the loss resurfaced; this was especially true when daughters became mothers themselves. As Maureen said, there was no manual to tell her how to be a mother and with the lack of a role model it was like being 'thrown in at the deep end'.

Motherhood was a role in which many daughters continued to 'cover their heart'. In reflecting on the role of a mother, daughters were influenced by their own experiences, of which grieving played a significant part. Daughters became acutely aware that their relationships with their own children were affected. The range of concerns included being the perfect mother, being over-protective and being able to express emotions to children. It is the latter that we explore first.

EXPRESSING EMOTIONS TO CHILDREN

In powerful and profound accounts, the women in the study shared honestly their deepest concerns about their relationships with their children. It was their belief that their ability to relate emotionally to their children was strongly influenced by the absence of their mother and the subsequent lack of affection in their lives.

With much emotion, Mary described how the loss of her mother, accompanied by the fact that displays of affection were not shown in her family, had impacted on her ability to show affection to her children. In sharing her story, Mary found herself wondering, if her mother had lived would things have been different:

> I cannot put my arms around even my own children now, even to this day. I could not say to them, 'I love you' and put my arms around them [pause – very emotional]. I think if my mother had been living she could have shown us that, I would have been able to have seen it.

Kathleen shared at length her concerns about her inability to relate emotionally to her children. She explained that when her children reached the age of ten, her insecurities 'kicked in' and her ability to relate well to them changed:

> I could communicate with the children right up until they were about ten. A strange age when I think about it now, but I was great with them, especially when they were babies. When their personalities started to change, when the children started to become a bit more independent and started to have opinions of their own and started to be able to chat – I didn't turn off the kids, it wasn't that, it was just me. My insecurities kicked in.
>
> I love them as much now as I did then, there's no change in me, but I can't show my emotions to them now. It's a struggle for me to show my deep feelings towards them. I see other parents, even going out in the morning they'd be kissing and cuddling their children, you know. I can't do it and [name of child] has said to me, 'You could be a bit more affectionate'. I can't do it and the children are suffering, I know they are, I know they are.

It is not surprising that, with their own mother-daughter relationship severed in early life, daughters (as mothers) were preoccupied with thoughts of their own experiences. It is not suprising that 'connecting' with children became difficult when daughters had so much of their own 'stuff' to process.

Is it possible for anyone who has lost someone significant in early life to have normal relationships with their own offspring, especially if they have not had the chance to openly mourn and grieve the loss? Might it be that unresolved feelings of grief so dominate the internal world that it prevents them from 'connecting' with those around them, even the people they love?

Kathleen's experience provoked such questions and in a sense helped us to speculate or go some way towards answering them. When her children reached the age she was when her mother died, she knew that from that age onwards she did not have her mother in her life, something she was more aware of (consciously and/or sub-consciously) than ever before. She was sensitive to the fact that her children had reached the stage of their lives that was a turning point in her own upbringing. Kathleen (and perhaps many others like her) was trying to cope with the residue of feelings that this landmark engendered – renewed feelings of loss, coping with the enormity of having missed out on a mother from the age of eleven onwards. At the same time she was trying to be open to her own children and their needs. Despite this, fear and dread took over. Kathleen didn't know what it was like to be mothered after the age of eleven and so she found herself in new territory and with it came the unexpected: emotional shutdown as the insecurities kicked in.

Dara explained that she hadn't really fully connected with her youngsters but she was sure that she was keeping 'that wee bit back just in case they die'. In the mind of an early bereaved daughter, the fear of further loss is very real. It is as if holding back is a buffer against the pain that would be re-experienced if a child died – a phenomenon that daughters, deeply sensitised to loss, experience.

Dara, whose situation was complicated by the fact that her first baby died when she was nineteen years old, explains that she 'hopes for the best but prepares for the worst'. If her children go out at night she lives in fear that something will happen to them. Her fear is that when they go out it may be the last time she will see them.

Even when contemplating motherhood (as noted by the youngest daughter in the study), Lesley was aware that motherhood might pose challenges. She voiced concerns about the possible impact of the legacy of loss:

> ... a big worry for me in the future – will I have post-natal depression if I ever have children? Will I suffer very badly? If I have a child of my own will there be this huge issue because I'll be thinking back, how did my mother feel, what happened, what did she experience?

We can imagine the dilemma that the early bereaved, as mothers, found themselves in. They loved their children and they wanted to be close to them but, having been scarred by their earlier loss, they found it difficult to get close to them. It was too risky. The questions in their mind were: if I allow myself to trust and get close, will history repeat itself? Will I lose someone I love again?

COMPENSATING FOR THE LACK OF LOVE

Some daughters, however, compensate for the lack of love in their own lives by furnishing their own children with an abundance of affection. There is a determination in daughters like Joanna and Helen, who have endured an abusive upbringing, to ensure that their children have a very different experience. Here's what they said:

> I think I try very hard. We never got any affection, never got a kiss, never got a hug. I'm always stroking and kissing and hugging and telling them how great they have done. I want them to know how much they are loved; maybe that is why I am doing it then. Making sure that, God forbid, if anything should happen, at least they know
> – Joanna.

It certainly hasn't prevented me from expressing emotions to them at all. I have a very good relationship with both the children. Coming from the background I did made me determined to bring my children up in a way that was so different to how we were brought up – Helen.

Elena too recognised that while there was consistent care during the years she was reared by her uncle and aunt, little affection was shown or expressed. She too was determined for things to be different:

With my own children, I was always hugging them and lifting them, things I had never experienced.

Regardless of the age of the child, many daughters admitted that, as mothers, they had a tendency to be over-protective and the inclination to do so was long-lasting. It was not something that was easily eradicated.

OVER-PROTECTIVE
Being over-protective was partly about the determination to make life comfortable for children, about 'being there' for them. Many, including Alison, Maureen, Patricia and Helen E, were unanimous about their protective feelings towards their children. Being sensitised to loss, such feelings come with the territory.

For example, Pauline was adamant that nobody has ever put her children to bed except her, and Maureen was always terrified letting them out. Here daughters provide clear evidence of the deeply cautious manner in which children were managed and protected. Patricia explained that her father wanted to make life as easy as possible for herself and her siblings after their mother died. So, in turn, she also wanted to 'move mountains' for her own children to ensure that they didn't worry needlessly about things and to make sure they weren't upset.

However, Alison discovered that 'survellience' strategies sometimes don't work with children as they get older. Her eighteen-year-old preferred not to be monitored by being called on her mobile phone, especially when she was out socially. Mothers can't help worrying even when children are older, as Helen E explained:

> If he went into the town at all I was just so hyped-up, so stressed out that I was even ending up having nightmares about it. They walk out that door at night and your heart is in your throat and you are afraid that something will happen to them. I'm sure most mothers are the same, you know.

Not all mothers branded themselves as over-protective, however. There were a few who took a different stance in relation to their children. Their own history of loss had shaped their thinking differently.

MAKING CHILDREN INDEPENDENT

Mary B was frank and clear in her philosophy of child-rearing. The fragility and uncertainty of life that had been demonstrated in her early years meant that she wanted to equip her offspring for the unpredictable journey ahead:

> My aim in life was to make my children independent because they didn't know how long their mother or their father were going to be there. That was very much in my mind.

Clare too was philosophical about the rearing of her boys. She seemed to take motherhood in her stride and tackled the role with a different attitude:

> I have two boys and they get covered in bumps and bruises and grazes and the people at the nursery say, 'It's as well you are not one of these mothers that overreact', because they always look like they have been through the wars.

Helen E revealed that her style of mothering was influenced by her own mother's more radical approach to life:

*I'm probably more open with the youngsters. The memories I have of
my mother is that she was someone who tried anything for a bit of
craic. I like to try to let the youngsters make up their own minds
about things and try different things.*

According to Ann, parents can be too diligent at times. She noted
that sometimes people need to be careful that they are not 'over-
supporting or over-protecting' children too much.

Part of the dilemma that daughters found themselves in was the
overwhelming desire to do the right thing in their own role as
mother; to put in a big effort for the children, to be 'there' for
them, to be 'perfect'.

The 'perfect mother'

Being motherless has helped to shape daughters' priorities. It was
the recognition that they now had a chance to give their children
what they had missed out on that became central in their lives. As
Ann said:

*The big thing missing in your life was your mother, so you wanted to
be the mother in the house with the children.*

Her message was that having a lot of money or a nice house was not
as important as being there for the children. The pressure of trying
to be perfect got to Dara:

*No matter how hard I try to be the perfect mother, it doesn't work; my
role as a mother has been one of my biggest hang-ups.*

It had a big effect on her when her son – at the age of six – said he
'hated' her for not allowing him to stay up past his bedtime. Even
though she realised that she shouldn't take it personally and that
he didn't mean it, it still hurt.

To serve the needs of her children, Pauline went to extremes.
Being creative and a talented seamstress she was able to produce
costumes from scratch. But the lack of recognition and appreciation
for such efforts caused her annoyance:

> *I am so motherly I would drive you crazy. It has to be the best costumes and they have to be made from scratch every single time. I'm very lucky that I can do that. But then I would be raging if they are not grateful – if they didn't appreciate it I would be so mad.*

Perhaps the subtext of Pauline's message was that the children should be appreciative of the fact that they do have their mother and that she was working hard to make life as good for them as possible. She was trying to be the best she could in the role.

What was clear from the stories and experiences so far was that very few parts of life remain untouched by the legacy of early bereavement. The loss etched itself so profoundly on the emotional landscape that all kinds of feelings erupted very readily despite efforts to cover up and protect the heart. The strongest and most deeply embedded were the fears that gripped daughters' lives. It was almost as if every aspect of life had fear attached to it. As we just saw above, the role of motherhood brought with it fears, tension and worry and that tapping into feelings around the death and loss brought fear to the surface. Daughters worried about many other things. They were sensitised to death and therefore an underlying fear of death featured heavily in their lives. In the words of Jennifer, when you are bereaved early in life 'the fear of loss is enhanced'.

When they encountered death, 'the harsh lesson' (as Maggie referred to it) at a young age, it had a profound effect on daughters' sense of safety and security. The world as they knew it was disrupted and dishevelled. Even if they were too young to know what death meant, they developed a fear of death and loss that remained with them endlessly.

Fear of death

Daughters' feelings about death were unmistakable, and in the interviews their fear was palpable at times. For some, thoughts about death were unbearable. For example, there was the fear of losing the other most significant person in their lives, their father; or the fear of approaching the age at which their mother died, in which case they thought they would die too; the deep enduring fear of dying in the same way their mother had or that their children would have to endure the same experience of loss. Such fears don't go away – they have to be endured (even to the present day) and they are difficult to eradicate. Hence, the psychological and physiological effects cannot be underestimated.

The development of these fears related to the relative silence within which daughters had grown up. As they navigated their way through life, their 'bottled up' thoughts and feelings found few avenues of emotional support. Therefore, in such circumstances – as might apply to anything in life – daughters came to their own conclusions about situations or events; trying to make sense of their internal emotional world was not easy.

For some, the feelings were difficult to overcome. Abbey described being 'absolutely petrified of death' and Mary said the loss of her mother had 'left a terrible fear of death'. When Theresa heard the priest speak of death in the chapel, she said it felt like there was a 'fist tightening in her stomach' (a phenomenon she still experiences to this day). The fear gripped her so intensely she said that she wanted to squeal to let it out.

Ann wanted to highlight that the fear of loss can transfer across the generations onto children who worry and fret about it. In her view, the child's thinking would be, 'if Mummy's mummy died when she was young, my mummy might die too'.

However, in providing evidence that she was not so absorbed with fears of death, Dara recalled a very profound conversation that she had with her mother about her own death:

> I don't have a fear of death, I'm not afraid to die, I would never have been afraid to die. I remember saying to my mammy, 'When I die can I take my blackboard to heaven?' She said, 'Well I'm sure God will

*have a blackboard in heaven, but if it makes you feel better I'll put a
wee blackboard in with you and you can take it with you'.*

Perhaps having had the unique opportunity for such a conversation
and the sensitivity and understanding shown by her mother helped
Dara's fears to diminish. However, for many early loss survivors,
fear of death and an expectation of dying were unavoidable features
in their lives.

FEAR OF REACHING THE LANDMARK AGE

Daughters have an insoluble fear of reaching the age their mother
was when she died because they think that they are doomed to die
then too. Some shared these real and deeply felt fears with their
female siblings. As the 'landmark' age looms, daughters are gripped
with a fear of dying: 'Next year is going to be full of angst when I get
to that age,' Anne confesses. The obsession was so powerful in
Abbey that it was present even though the death of her mother at
thirty-four was as the result of an accidental fall. Abbey is
convinced, however, that she might die prematurely:

> My mum was only thirty-four when she died and I think I have a very
> great fear that something similar is going to happen to me, or that I
> will not see thirty-five, and that is a fear.

When she was within a year of the age at which her mother died,
Clare wondered, introspectively, what it would be like if this was 'her
last year of life'. This was the question she posed herself when she
found herself in that age zone. It is as if she is putting herself in her
mother's shoes and looking at life through a different lens.

However, daughters did more than speculate on the prospect of
death. Even though she admitted having no fear of death, Dara was so
convinced that history would repeat itself, i.e. she was going to die at
thirty-one, the same as her mother and maternal grandmother had, she
made her will and funeral arrangements in her thirty-first year. When
she didn't die, she felt guilty that she was 'on this earth' longer than her

mother had been and she deliberated on the fact that she had more children than her mother had. She poses herself the question:

What right did I have to be alive longer; she had to die when she was thirty-one?

But when she 'escaped' death at thirty-one, Dara took a second chance at life by returning to education.

At specific times or during specific life events (such as pregnancy and childbirth), maternally bereaved daughters were extremely conscious of the cause of their mother's death. They became sensitised to the fact that, if this was how their mother died or if something in particular caused her death, then it might happen the same way for them too.

FEAR OF DYING IN THE SAME WAY

In the same way that daughters were extremely sensitive to age, the way in which their mother died also caused extreme anxiety and an alertness about their own health. They anticipate that they will die in the same way or for the same reason. This is particularly true when the death occurred as a result of childbirth. When Mary was expecting her children she said:

That was the time that I prayed the hardest, please God don't let me die.

However, her prayers did not stop there. As her children reached each religious event (communion, confirmation), she continued to plead with God that she would live to see the next significant event.

The desire to keep a check on health was driven by the knowledge of the cause of death. For example, Elaine's awareness that her mother developed deep vein thrombosis enabled her to make a decision about smoking and taking the pill.

Kathleen's mother died of cancer and she became obsessive about her health. When the turning point of forty arrived, panic set in:

I would be a bit obsessed about cancer after Mammy had cancer. I would tend to be a bit of a hypochondriac about my health generally, especially about cancer. I'm forty now, and I'm starting to get panicky about it and conscious of my diet, because Mammy didn't have a good diet.

People may not have been aware at the time, but that when inaccurate information was passed on about the cause of death, it stuck. This was the case even when the truth was realised in later years. Dara's testimony below reinforced the notion that young children need the truth. They need to be given accurate information about the death (that matches their age and level of understanding):

We were told at the time that she ate a tin of spaghetti that was off. I found out then when I was about sixteen it was actually septicaemia she died from. She had an ingrown toenail that had festered and she got blood poisoning. For years nobody in our family ate spaghetti, you know, my brothers and sisters, none of us would touch spaghetti. It seems like a wee silly detail, even still as an adult it seems like a real big thing. Even though I know it wasn't the spaghetti, it's the thing that sticks in my head.

FEAR OF LOSING CHILDREN

Daughters were both sensitive to and threatened by the issue of death. It was almost as if they were on high alert because the experience of loss in early life had imprinted a message that death can occur quite suddenly and unexpectedly. Being so 'tuned' to loss led to insidious thoughts of death, and daughters' sensitivities were exacerbated when the funerals of friends' mothers or people whom they were close to had to be attended.

In emphasising her feelings about losing people or losing a child, Jennifer admitted that she had a dreadful fear of the worst happening. Life was overshadowed with a fear of loss that other people, who were not sensitised in the same way, may not think about.

FEAR OF HISTORY REPEATING ITSELF

An early experience of loss was a legacy that daughters hoped would not be bestowed on their own children. But one of their strongly held fears was that history would repeat itself. As they talked through their own life story– the loss of a mother, the loss of a family unit and being thrust into a new and different life situation – they admitted to deep fears and concerns that their children would have to endure the same as they went through. The dread was that children would have to face a life situation where they would lose the family unit and be thrust into a situation where 'things weren't the same' – a scenario that the early bereaved knew only too well. It was not only the worry of children having to endure the same life script, it was also that daughters wanted to have good health so that they could live to see them grow up.

FEAR OF TALKING ABOUT THE LOSS AND 'CLICKING INTO FEELINGS'

Talking about emotional issues in life is never easy. Sometimes we put on a brave front and talk at a superficial level to hide our true feelings. Daughters were in a continual state of anxiety, fearful that their mother's death would come up in conversation. Anticipating that it might 'come out' was enough to instill fear.

In order to manage their feelings when talking about their mother, daughters relied on the tactic of 'disconnecting' in order to avoid the emotions that they knew would be difficult to cope with (especially in front of someone else). Dara explained how she 'rescued' herself in a situation:

> I can talk about her but, you see, if I click into my feelings while I'm talking about her I would be in bits, so I can kind of make that disconnection, if you like.

When a doctor commiserated unexpectedly with Lesley, she felt 'mortified and embarrassed'. On a routine visit, he opened her medical file and said: 'I see your mother died. When did she die? It must have been very difficult for you and for your father.' The sudden introduction to her history of loss and the sympathy shown by her caring doctor left Lesley feeling very vulnerable. It wasn't that she didn't appreciate the concern shown to her, but the difficult part was the fear of having to talk because it was 'painful' and also because she didn't know 'anything about it' to be able to discuss it. 'Don't mention the war!' she quipped with a smile. Little wonder that her main wish in that moment was to get out of the surgery because the last thing Lesley (and all early bereaved daughters) want is for the floodgates to open in front of someone else.

Daughters prefer to find a private space where they can release their emotions. Joanna confided that:

> I don't like people seeing how I am really feeling; I take myself off into a wee corner and lick my wounds.

Abbey agrees:

> When I am feeling upset I don't like to show it, not outwardly. If I do want to have a good cry, it's usually behind closed doors.

For the early bereaved in the present day, the subject of loss may still be too raw and emotionally unmanageable to talk about. Survivors want to hide their emotions or at best manage them out of the view of others. They prefer that others not see how they are feeling. It takes awareness and sensitivity to remember that the impact of the loss on the psyche is lifelong and can erupt at any time.

FEAR OF BEING ALONE

Daughters' lives were a recipe for the development of fear, dread and an insidious sense of insecurity. As they had lived a life overshadowed by isolation and loneliness in their growing-up years, now more than ever, being alone was an unwelcome state – one they wanted to avoid. As adults, daughters preferred the company of people to aloneness. Being alone was a precursor for hypervigilance in Lesley:

I would have a great fear of being on my own. If I am alone in the house I don't like it; I would be quite a jumpy person.

Maureen summed up the preferred scenario in a simple direct statement: 'I love people around me.'

FEAR OF BEING FORGOTTEN

From the perspective of maternally bereaved daughters who knew what it was like to live in a climate of silence and secrecy about their mothers, the fear of being forgotten almost became an obsession. Having lived a life characterised by the loss of a mother and now in the role of mother with their own children, daughters were deeply aware of their desire and need to be remembered. In their own lives they had struggled with the lack of information, the lack of discussion and a general climate in which remembering their own mothers was almost disallowed. Therefore, the fear of being forgotten played heavily on daughters' minds. Helen admitted that her fear of being forgotten was close to paranoia:

I was always very anxious that if anything happened to me [tearful] that my children wouldn't be allowed to forget me.

In her testimony, Joanna had stated that she had only one fleeting memory of her mother, who died when she was three. She remembered her mother handing her a Mars bar as she stood at the living-room window. As she reflected on her own three-year-old and the richness of their life together, she voiced her fears. Joanna estimated that, should she die now, her three-year-old would not remember her, a sentiment she conveyed with sadness in her voice:

She is only three and I was three when I lost my mammy. I think how much me and her go through together every day and the banter. If I died she wouldn't remember me and that is really hurtful; I couldn't bear the thought that she wouldn't remember me if I was to die now.

Perhaps the scant memories that were available to those whose mothers had died when they were very young informed them that, should they die, the likelihood was they would not be remembered, unless others took steps to make sure that they would never be forgotten.

Growing up, daughters found that there were many painful emotions brought to the surface but concealed from others.

JEALOUSY

It was difficult for daughters to observe others with parents in a 'normal' family setting – 'there was a mammy and daddy and everything was rosy' – and to accept that they no longer had the same opportunity:

> There's a bit of jealousy that other people have parents.

Maggie felt the same way about her situation. She was reared separately from her siblings, who were brought up in the family home:

> As I got older I used to be jealous of my brothers and sisters because they were reared together in my father's house and I used to be jealous of that.

In very moving accounts, daughters illustrated and confirmed that the untimely loss of their mother had shaped and changed their lives, including their mental, emotional and physical health. As we will see presently, the 'breaking of the bond' contributed to psychological disturbances such as anxiety, stress and depression. The struggle began in the early years and continues in the present day, but it became clear also that not everyone holds the same view about depression and its triggers. It comes down to individuality – people with different experiences and different views.

PROPENSITY TOWARDS DEPRESSION AND ILLNESS

From an early age, bereaved daughters suffered symptoms of anxiety and depression; the symptoms varied in depth, intensity and onset. Pauline, whose mother died when she was eight, recognised that within a couple of years she was struggling with her mental health. Here she described how it manifested in early life and then in later life:

> I remember having symptoms of depression from when I was ten really. You hear people talking about this black hole and you can't get out of it. That is very real.

> I suffer from terrible anxiety. I was actually in coronary care for two days. I thought I'd had a heart attack. But it was palpitations and the way they explained it on paper was, 'abnormal awareness of irregular heartbeat'. Just pure stress, and a thing I have never been able to shake.

Louise's mother died when she was just under two years old. She recalled with sadness how she felt in the early years:

> Looking back as a child I had depression as a result of my own mother dying and circumstances changing. In school I was very withdrawn and found it very hard to form relationships with people. I had a lot of anxiety inside of me even as a young child.

And she went on to describe how the loss had impacted in the longer term:

> I'm on anti-depressants at the minute. I was always quite anxious. There were times when I couldn't be bothered getting out of bed and not knowing why. But when I look back I think that it actually was in childhood as well. As an adult, I developed athsma and thyroid disease, depression and always had troubles with period cramps and pains and heavy periods, so I am on medication for that as well. I do feel that this has to do with all that stress throughout my life.

While some daughters attribute their mental and emotional difficulties to their mother's death and the ramifications that followed, there were those who suggested that other life events triggered off their depression. In thought-provoking words, Maggie explained how the change in her mental health came about in her thirties. For her, it was following the death of two significant people who had been caring for her throughout her life and the termination of a long-term relationship that depression set in:

> In my thirties my [name of relative] died and my [name of relative] died. At the same time I had ended a long-term relationship – I went into a real depression. My long-term friend – we would have known each other since we were four – I remember distinctly telling her that death is just here on my shoulder. Not so depressed that I had to be clinically treated but I did go to a psychotherapist. I certainly realised that I will always have a propensity towards depression.

Kathleen had always suffered loneliness and unhappiness in her early years. But when she was diagnosed with epilepsy in her twenties, depression followed. However, she was unable to take prescribed drugs for both conditions as, taken together, one would have cancelled out the other. In the end she sought counselling:

> When I was about twenty-six I developed epilepsy. I'm still considered an epileptic but it's controlled now. I'm still on drugs at the minute. It was about seven years before they got it controlled and then I did develop depression about five years ago. I went to the psychologist and he said it was definitely clinical depression, but he couldn't put me on anti-depressants because of the epilepsy tablet: one negated the other.

Alison was convinced that the depression she suffered was not only related to 'all those years ago', and that periods of unemployment and the break-up of her marriage were attributable to the bouts of depression she experienced. In Joanna's case, depression was diagnosed in the aftermath of a car crash. At the time of the interview her mood had improved, but there remained an emotionality that was never far away, especially when things did not go well. However, she had the propensity to bounce back:

> I had a car crash and depression followed it. I was referred out to a GP for the whiplash and when we were going through everything he said, 'You know, I think you are depressed'. I still get upset and cry

*now and again when things don't go well. I panic easy. If things are
not going according to how I have planned them, but I wouldn't call
it a breakdown, but I crumble and then I think, right, how do we get
this back on track.*

However, alternative views about the experience of depression came
to light in the testimonies. Not everyone could or would admit to
depression, even when the symptoms were felt. Karen had the
feeling that she was suffering with depression but she didn't want
to admit to it. The resistance she felt may correspond to Dara's
belief that depression was a weakness, therefore to be avoided at all
costs. Rather than allow herself to get depressed, Dara used the
strategy of cutting off her emotions to avoid getting down:

*I have never suffered from depression. I wouldn't allow myself. I
always saw people who were depressed or needed to get medication for
depression as a weakness. I know that it's not, but I would never
allow myself to get into that state – back to that cut-off thing again.*

Liz's view on the topic of depression included the rationale that
there were people she knew who had experienced more positive
circumstances in life who were very depressed. As she observed, if
others had a good family home and they still got 'very depressed'
then the events of upbringing was not a sole reason for the
development of depression. She reflected:

*I would have known people in circumstances that were considerably
less difficult than mine who had perfectly good family homes and who
were very depressed.*

This served as a reminder to us all that we can look at another's life,
observe it to be positive and therefore assume that all is well. When
we learn that the person suffers with bouts of anxiety or depression
we wonder how this can be when their life circumstances seem so
good. Daughters teach us that we need to hold judgement when
viewing others because we don't know enough about them. It was
not good for early bereaved adult daughters to be observed in later

years by others who assumed that, since they were older, they should be over the loss of their mother, since it happened a long time ago!

Children (depending on their age) do not have the ability to understand that death is permanent. When daughters were young and attached to their mother, they didn't have the reasoning or intuition to understand *why* she was no longer there, but instinctively they knew things had changed and they missed her. The loss of her was an event that brought with it the *distress* of separation that caused not only psychological effects, but physical effects also.

In the months after her mother died, Louise suffered the pernicious effects of stress in the form of depression and many other health problems:

> When my mother died I was only about a year and nine months. About six months after she died I developed double pneumonia. The doctors at the time believed that it was a form of distress because I was separated from my mother and my immune system had decreased and I was now prone to infections. I was very ill with double pneumonia along with rheumatic heart fever as well. There was this bond and it was broken. I was the one she was nursing in her arms constantly. Literally the day before she died they had to take me out of her arms.

It needs to be remembered that for those who have experienced early adversity, a vulnerability remains afterwards that may remain dormant, unrealised until other life situations are encountered that can trigger off a new cycle of grief.

FRIENDS AND FAMILY

Despite the emotional, mental and physical demands on their health, daughters found ways and means of coping. They developed resources and ways of managing their emotions that many others who have experienced early loss will be aware of. Comfort was sought and found through the support and help of lifelong friends and family members, as explained by Jennifer, Theresa, Ann and others. It was friendship, being afforded the opportunity to talk, being accepted and being cared about that seemed to be fruitful resources:

> *I have good friends and I have a brother and his wife and his children – I would be closer to them than I would my own family. I have more or less grown up with them so I am very, very close to them and we would talk about absolutely anything. There's that bond there and I think that contributed a lot. The few people that care about you, they can put a different slant on things for you; completely different slant. Even though they haven't gone through it themselves, they look to me as someone who has* – Theresa.

> *I have two very good friends who have been there for twenty-two years* – Jennifer.

> *I suppose maybe in one way myself and [name of sister] are very close, maybe we were lucky that there was two of us and we were able to support each other. I know we are too close, fighting, squabbling and all the rest of it, but I suppose in a strange way we were able to replace that mother bond with each other* – Ann.

The impact of the early loss of a mother and the legacy it bequeaths will not leave survivors unscathed. The significant 'blow' was an enormous challenge to young daughters' emotional health, mental health and well-being.

It was important to daughters that others realise that when someone bereaved in early life reaches adulthood, they have not automatically recovered from the loss. Time creates a distance and while they may not be lapsing into raw grief every day, the emotional wound may not have healed. It was for this reason that daughters, indeed, found the need to cover their hearts and protect themselves. However, coming 'out of the wilderness' and participating in the study helped daughters to end the silence and, in doing so, enable others to know what it means to endure early loss.

6. 'HE WAS A VERY GOOD FATHER'

He was a very good father. If we hadn't had a good father,
I don't know what we would have done – Maude.

If we were to stop and consider the plight of a family who is bereaved of a mother, we would surely be conscious of the devastation that the loss brings to both the adults and children. A black cloud descends and looms over everything and everyone. Kathleen's recollection helps us to understand what that might be like and how the loss can change the family home:

> *Everything went serious, the mood changed, the colour changed. We used to come home from school and it was just sombre.*

Instead of drawing the family closer together (as some expected it might or should have done), it pulls some households apart. Abbey said it pulled her family apart because no-one in her family talked about their feelings or admitted their feelings. As in most homes, her mother was a 'closed subject'.

But daughters knew that the adults had suffered a tremendous blow. The pain of grief felt by fathers was something the children silently witnessed in the months and years following the loss. Daughters sensed that their fathers couldn't talk, they didn't want to talk or they got upset when they did talk.

It was a hard struggle for the remaining parent to cope; not only were they dealing with their own grief, but they had young bereaved children in grief. As Alison firmly conveyed:

> *He couldn't deal with it himself, so how could he help three kids deal with it?*

The intense emotional impact of the death rendered fathers unable to discuss the loss. In the midst of the emotional turmoil and disarray, fathers were not coping. It was a deeply unhappy time and fathers literally may not have been able to speak for days and weeks. They were preoccupied and distant, steeped in grief, as Lesley realised:

> My father is so caring but he doesn't have the ability to pass on or express anything about my mother.

When their father got upset that was the most difficult time. As a result, daughters learned that the only way to 'protect' their father's feelings was to not ask questions. Their aim was to protect their father from emotional pain. In retrospect, it was explained that it could have been that being 'regimented' in their outlook or reared to muster a 'stiff upper lip' in times of hardship determined how some fathers responded. But daughters sensed that it was coping with the emotional pain of the loss and not knowing how to talk to the youngsters that had 'silenced' their fathers.

In the interviews there were those who spoke positively about the role their fathers had played in their lives. While he may not have been able to offer emotional support, daughters recognised that he had tried his best to support the family in whatever way he could. These were also fathers who did not have another relationship or who did not allow another relationship to interfere in family life. It was fathers who were consistently there and who tried to create a sense of normality that daughters revered. When a father is absolutely gutted, recovery is slow. While Patricia proudly reported, 'My father would have moved mountains rather than upset us', she was also very cognisant of the fact that he never recovered from the loss:

> Part of him died that night as well; he never got over it.

'THERE WAS NOTHING THERE FOR DADDY TO HELP HIM'

Alison's happy family life changed the day that her mother died in a car accident in which they were all involved. As she compassionately reflected on her father, Alison was clear that he was a good provider in terms of material things. While she recognised that he wasn't able to support the family emotionally, she was also adamant that there was little help available for him:

> It was hard emotionally because my mum wasn't there. But there was nothing there for Daddy to help him – how do you talk to kids who have just lost a mother?

Following the death of her mother from cancer when Theresa was eleven years old, she found it 'very tough' that her father couldn't talk about her mother. But she knew he was in emotional pain:

> I really found it very, very tough because Daddy wouldn't have talked about her. I think he was hurting that much himself he just wasn't able to talk about her. If he had started to talk about her, he would have burst out crying. She just wasn't discussed.

Ann's mother died in childbirth and she felt that this was a double blow to her father. He was traumatised:

> Any time Daddy started talking about her, he got so upset. The baby died when she died, so he never really wanted to talk about it. Obviously it was a very traumatic time and he never wanted to bring it up.

Elena's mother died two weeks after she was born. Her father couldn't cope and other family members had to come to the rescue. In the end, her aunt and uncle (her father's brother) became carers to Elena and her older brother. The enormity of the task undertaken and the humanity shown by her relatives was respected and appreciated as the years passed:

> You see, Daddy lost heart when she died. He couldn't carry on. He just went to pieces and my uncle stepped in and took us. My uncle was very good because he took another man's two children and reared them. He was a great man.

Inside, a young bereaved child holds many worries, fears and anxieties that are sparked by the death of their mother. When they experience such an ordeal, the child then puts a lot of stake in the remaining parent – a new level of importance is placed upon a father. But children soon begin to fear that he might die too.

ATTACHED TO DADDY

The 'harsh lesson', as Maggie defined it, had taught daughters about life and loss; it created in them a fear of losing the one other significant adult person who remained – their father. Ann articulated how she 'transferred' everything to her father and how he became extremely important in her life:

> I was so traumatised that I automatically attached myself to Daddy then. I seemed to transfer to Daddy, so I would have been very attached to him. What was normal for me was Daddy being there and us being there.

Even when there are no particular signs of ill health, bereaved children can develop a premature fear and concern about their fathers. Lesley illustrated this when she began talking about her fears:

> I do have a fear now that he's going to die or wonder about when he's going to die. I mean, he's not an ill person – he wouldn't be particularly healthy, but he doesn't have any chronic conditions or any history of bad health. But I would have a fear about what's going to happen when he dies, that it will be very bad because I will be an orphan. I think of it that way – I will be an orphan.

Even though it was many years before her father passed away, Theresa so dreaded the thought of losing him as well that she mourned his death for many years before it happened.

> The fear I had of losing him was something else. I would have mourned his death years before he ever died with the fear of losing him.

Jennifer's plea was that others would recognise the insecurity felt by bereaved children around the well-being of the remaining parent. Over the years she had established a pattern of worrying about her father, but it was an insecurity that was silently endured:

> It needs to be recognised how insecure children feel as a result of losing a parent. I can remember having a terrible, terrible fear that something was going to happen to my father, dreadful, you know. When he started going out at night, I would be left waiting, actually tossing and turning in bed until I would hear him coming home. Sometimes it wasn't until two in the morning but I would be awake. But that went on for years and years and years.

'IN MY EYES HE IS A SAINT'

Daughters were grateful for the fathers or father figures they had. Dara spoke of the importance of the 'father figure' who had been part of her life for many years, and as noted above, Elena admired the qualities of her father's brother who had provided herself and her brother with a stable home.

Somehow, the lack of emotional support was mediated by the fact that fathers/father figures were consistently there and devoted themselves to their families. Helen E summed up her feelings of gratitude towards her father:

> I think that that security I had: my daddy is there, we are not going to split up, we are going to be OK. He probably had the biggest influence on me from that point of view and also because I am incredibly proud of what he done. In my eyes he is a saint – we had great summer holidays and everything else.

Maude said that she was reassured by her older sister that things would work out for the family:

> My eldest sister said, 'You are not to worry because we have a good father and I'm standing in as your mother'.

Maude realised that her sister was right:

> *He was a very good father; if we hadn't had a good father I don't know what we would have done.*

However, she went on to acknowledge that it wasn't possible to be worry-free, especially when she began talking about her brother:

> *My brother went to sea after my mother died. He seemed to want to get away. I think he had to get away. I think maybe it affects boys dreadfully.*

The strength of a father's devotion and the role he played in providing consistency, love, security and comfort was recalled by Patricia:

> *I know I have missed out on a lot but my father was always a great comfort. I think my father became two parents, although he was quiet and reserved. He was my daddy and he was there. It was strange my father making dinner. He was great. My father made life as easy as possible for us. He would have moved mountains rather than upset us.*

Perhaps the input from bereaved daughters at the conference in London helps us to understand the concept that if a father does not remarry or allow another relationship to interfere in family life, then a daughter feels she doesn't have to 'compete' with that person for her father's attentions.

Like Patricia's father, Ann's father took over the parenting role and tried to make things as normal as possible for the family. Elizabeth too fondly recalled her father's nature and personality:

> *Daddy was a very, very kind and good person; sometimes, I always say, he was nearly too soft.*

Mary knew that her father's outlook on life was not the same as hers, but she appreciated that he looked after the family well:

> *He was one of those men that was old-fashioned. He was a very good provider.*

When the father figure that Dara had known for years was wrenched out of her life, it was a traumatic end to a relationship that had become very important to the young members of the family. Dara said that she was able to retain him mentally in 'this wee box' and in later years she was able to maintain a relationship from a distance. But the loss of him at the time was like a 'double blow':

> [Name] was the first father figure we actually had because my mother and father has split up when we were really young. Me and [name of sibling] especially adored him. I think it was that girl and the daddy thing and that's something that has lasted to this day. Because as we got older and left home we kept in touch with [name], but it was traumatic and it's something that never goes away. It's something that is always there so you try and keep it in this wee box, keep it over there and you don't think about it.

The loss had taken its toll on the emotional health and well-being of fathers. Their futures too were devastated and forever changed by the loss. Daughters recognised that the years following the death of their mother were turbulent for everyone in the family. Therefore, fathers who became two parents, who took over the complete parenting role and tried to create some sense of normality, were highly regarded and very much appreciated.

CONCLUSION
THE 'INCALCULABLE' LOSS

*It is incalculable how the loss of a mother just bereaves someone who
is growing up* – Jennifer.

The breadth and depth of the loss and the secondary losses that the
untimely death of a mother invokes can hardly be imagined,
especially for those who have observed rather than experienced the
event. It is an event, as Louise confirms, that *changes the whole course*
of life. No matter how hard we might try to put ourselves in the
shoes of someone who has lived with such adversity, it remains
difficult to fully comprehend what it would be like to come through
the experience. When we witness the impact of early loss (or other
types of adversity that people endure in early life) on those who are
close to us, we can see the devastating blow it is and the indelible
mark it leaves. The loss of a mother in early life remains a 'live' issue
in the hearts and minds of survivors.

It is important at this point to convey that, in the interview, when
Jennifer expressed the sentiment, 'It is incalculable how the loss of a
mother just bereaves someone who is growing up', the words were
spoken slowly and deliberately with depth of feeling. It is as if to
emphasise that the loss impacts so pervasively in the life of a
developing child that its effects are virtually impossible to measure.

Throughout their lives, daughters continually yearn for their
mother – the inescapable loss is never far away from the surface.
Everything in life holds a different meaning because, as time goes
on, the deep and lasting implications of the death and loss of a
mother are realised.

Here, in this final chapter, as daughters reflect on the meaning and overall impact of the loss, their thoughts and insights help to deepen our understanding of what it is like to have lived in the shadow of loss and how the reverberations are, indeed, deep and long-lasting. In heartfelt words, daughters shared their reflections about the lived experience of growing up without their mother. As they reviewed how life was and is without their mothers, daughters were wistful in their reflections. They recognised and realised that, as a result of their untimely deaths, mothers too had 'missed out' in life; silence and grieving remained open-ended; the loss had sensitised them to others (adults and children) in their grief and influenced them in their work roles. However, while the untimely death and loss had left an indelible mark, there were those who offered their personal philosophies that had evolved across their lifetime. Some spoke of feeling 'lucky', reclaiming control and moving on – indications of a new understanding and acceptance.

REFLECTIONS ON MUM – 'SHE MISSED OUT'

Daughters expressed with sadness and regret that through their early deaths, mothers had missed out on life. The opportunity to see the family growing up into adulthood was denied to them. As Anne said:

> I look and I think, she has missed all this, she has missed that we became people that she would be proud of.

Clare's regret was that her mother lost out on the chance for a new start in a new home:

> When Mum was ill we had been making plans to move – building a new bungalow – I was sorry that she missed out and never saw that.

Early bereaved daughters can be burdened with guilt about their mothers' deaths, as in the case of Louise. She felt deeply about the fact that her mother had borne nine children and then died at the age of thirty-seven:

Growing up, just thinking about her circumstances, I felt guilt that she had nine of us and then died so young. I felt guilt that she didn't have to have us.

Louise's acknowledgement of the guilt she lives with might help others to know and understand that such feelings can be part of life for the early bereaved. People looking on may regard such feelings as futile, but to daughters they are real and it is they, in their own time, who have to find ways of alleviating them.

Daughters were not only concerned about the impact on their personal welfare, they also recognised that their children were missing out on the experience of having a grandmother. The family unit that was disrupted so early in life was severely missed.

GRANDCHILDREN MISSING OUT

The legacy of the loss transfers itself across the generations. The fact that children would never know their grandmother was lamented, as described by Anne:

You know it's there, just a huge loss, and I feel it now that my sons will never know her.

It especially hit home when youngsters saw their friends going off to visit or stay with their grandparents. Alison had the positive experience of a grandmother and when she listened to her children bemoaning a granny to go and visit, she yearned for the close family unit that was absent:

I really miss the close family unit because my two children are missing out on a grandmother. In fact, they are missing out on a grandmother on both sides. I have lovely memories of going to visit my grandmother, you know. That's what I would love, to have that nice close family unit. I crave that family unit.

THE GAP REMAINS: 'HER LOSS WILL NEVER LEAVE ME'

In lives that had been irrevocably changed, the void, the missing and the gap seemed destined to remain. Daughters were aware that their lives were forever changed; what was lost could not be restored. It was the 'nurturing, security and unconditional love' – the lifeblood of the developing child – that was craved. Anne summarises:

> I think the mother is the provider of most nurturing. There is a huge gap; there always will be a huge gap.

Helen E succinctly summarised the history and legacy bestowed upon daughters and confirmed that the significant and lifelong impact of the loss was there to stay:

> Her loss will never leave me. It's not in my head every minute of the day, every day of the week, but there are times that it definitely is there very strong. It does have a significant impact and it always will.

Maureen too found that it was impossible to avoid reminders of being motherless:

> I am very aware of not having a mother when I hear people talking about mothers in different roles, because mothers by their nature play a very important role in society.

In a few heartfelt words, Dara profoundly captured what had been missing in her life from the age of ten onwards. She said:

> I've always missed not having somebody to call Mammy.

Elena's search for what was missing continues, but, as she discovers, her efforts are fruitless:

> To this day you are still missing. Even to this day you are always looking for something. It's hard to explain but there is that something missing and you can never replace it.

Theresa unequivocally states her view as she reminds us that emotions can be suspended in time and that time does not necessarily heal grief. When security and (unconditional) love virtually disappear, she vows that healing is difficult:

It's as raw as the day it happened. You just have a different upbringing and you haven't that security of a mother's love and somebody who loves you unconditionally no matter what you do.

So profound was the impact of the death that it continues to infiltrate daughters' thinking and emotions. To be able to work through any traumatic event in life, we have to be able to express how we feel when we are ready and able to do so. If this doesn't happen, the event can remain unresolved. Within daughters, a never-ending residue of emotions remain and the search for meaning is open-ended.

'I'M JUST STARTING TO ASK QUESTIONS'

We saw in an earlier chapter that taking part in the study was the *first time* that Karen had spoken about the death and loss of her mother that occurred twenty-six years ago. It was also notable that, at the time, taking part was an ambition that she had not shared, even with her husband. However, being unaccustomed to talking about the experience of loss with others was not a deterrent to taking part in the study.

But what Karen's experience represents is the continuation of the climate of silence that had presided over the death and loss of mothers. It has remained a feature of many daughters' lives to the present day. The death was earmarked by silence for such a long time that communicating, even with those closest, was difficult and finding out information was laborious. Theresa admits that she has begun to ask questions again after many years of silence:

Even yesterday I was asking questions about her: how long she suffered for? When did she die? I'm just starting to ask questions now because nobody really talks about her.

This glimpse into the present day confirms that little has changed, but it also shows that the need to know will force daughters into unchartered territory.

Regardless of how far society has come in addressing issues of death, loss and grief, people still struggle. Perhaps talking about death is uncomfortable as it confronts the individual with a reminder of their own immortality. While daughters appreciate that people become 'ill at ease and uncomfortable' when death is mentioned, the unanimous decision is that 'it should be something that you talk about'. This is the answer to daughters' prayers – that people would talk about the death and loss because bereaved children *need to know*, they need accurate information, they need help and emotional support from adults to enable them to grieve.

THOUGHTS ABOUT GRIEVING: 'YOU HAVE LEARNED WHAT IT IS TO LOSE'

An interesting range of views emerged as daughters unveiled their thoughts and feelings about the loss. The general sense conveyed by daughters is that grief is an ongoing part of life, a continuum on which they are to remain indefinitely. For some, accepting the loss seems to become more and more difficult as the years pass. Some have begun the grieving process while, for others, adjusting to the loss is an insurmountable task that may never be accomplished, as Helen E confirmed:

> *I suppose it's silly to say that I have not grieved for her after all these years, but I don't know if you ever fully get over it, I really don't.*

The depth of grief about the loss of that special close relationship that is possible between mother and child is captured in the heartfelt words:

> *What I grieve for is the intimacy of a mother.*

Maggie went on to disclose that she has searched for meaning through psychotherapy and that she has really only begun the grieving process in her thirties:

> *I don't think I have fully grieved her loss. I think I have to some extent in my thirties, certainly with very good friends and a support system. It's only in my thirties that I realised that I had a right to grieve that loss.*

Maggie's mother died when she was five months old and she was reared by her maternal grandparents and aunt. When their deaths occurred, Maggie (then in her thirties) said that this was the time she felt the personal loss of a mother. The deaths of those who had cared for her growing up seemed to bestow on her a sense of having a 'right to grieve'. It was as if a psychological path was cleared, allowing the full impact of loss to hit home, and with it the right to grieve.

Louise had a similar experience to Maggie when her stepmother died:

> *I think when my stepmother died I started to accept my own mother's death better.*

Interestingly, a knock-on effect of the death was that the ritual of mentally selecting a mother figure, which was a big part of Louise's life for many years, ended. She found that when it was possible for her to really begin to grieve the loss of her natural mother, she didn't feel the need to search for 'replacements' in her life.

Some had views about age at the time of the death and its impact on the loss. Liz was five months old when her mother died, and she argued that it wasn't possible to grieve because her mother was 'unknown to her':

> *I have never grieved for my mother because I didn't know her. She simply never existed for me and that is still how I feel.*

The concept that a mother who was not known and therefore never existed can remain firmly fixed in the mind of a bereaved daughter. Perhaps others reading this will concur with Liz in this view. So, the question is, how does a daughter who lost her mother in the first months of life begin the process of accepting her mother's existence and grieving her loss? Surely the answer must be continuous support and encouragement from adults to honour a mother's memory through talking about her, retaining keepsakes like pictures or artefacts that hold a special meaning.

Ann, who was bereaved at the age of five, seemed certain that it might have been even more traumatic for children to lose their mother when they are more aware of what is going on. Elaine partly agrees:

> Had I been a teenager when I lost my mum, I think it would have had a bigger impact on me. Maybe the impact is more subtle and more subconscious, though it is still a loss, it's still as equal a loss no matter what age you are. The only thing is you have learned what it is to lose. If you are that bit older I would say it would be more of a wrench.

However, Elaine found it impossible to delve into the full meaning of the loss. She was sure that if the enormity of the loss was to be realised it could cause her great distress; therefore to avoid such an outcome she preferred not to think:

> I wouldn't like to think because I think I would get upset if I realised how big the loss is.

This was followed by a long pause. The pause at this point in the interview spoke volumes. It was as if expressing her feelings out loud inadvertently triggered the thinking process that Elaine was trying to avoid. She remained quiet and pensive for a period of time afterwards. It was not a moment that could be interrupted or questioned.

'YOU CAN UNDERSTAND WHERE PEOPLE ARE COMING FROM'

The deeply profound loss of a mother in early life created sensitivity and understanding towards adults and children who struggled with the pain of loss or separation. Earlier in the book, Kathleen showed how her experience of loss helped her in her role as a teacher. In the course of their lives and in their careers, daughters were able to apply the knowledge and insight gained from their experiences. Having lived a life signified by loss (that was deeply engrained in their psyche), daughters were especially attuned to pain and loss when it was present. They were able to draw on their personal experience of loss to offer support and help when people were in need. For example, when Ann was working as a nurse it meant that death and dying was a common feature of the job. Knowing what it feels like to lose a loved one enabled her to help others. She explains in detail how she utilises her experience in her professional role and in voluntary work to facilitate others:

> *Because you are dealing with people dying, you are able to give. You can give more because you can understand where people are coming from. Instead of saying I know how you feel, you can say, I really know how you feel because I lost my mammy when I was young, and you can sort of use that to help other people in a way.*

Ann was quite taken with the fact that others who opted to train as facilitators of parenting courses were early loss survivors:

> *Doing a lot of parenting classes has helped because it is the first thing that has made me stop and think. Being able to talk to outsiders has actually been a great help because you had to talk about how you were parented. But it is amazing how people on that course had either lost a mother or a father very young. There was an awful lot of us when you went around the group; we all had quite traumatic experiences with the loss of a parent at a young age.*

What seems evident here is that the lived experience of loss (and its ramifications) had resulted in a changed perspective. Having the ability to understand 'where people are coming from' represents growth and change that is manifested in sensitivity and compassion and the ability to reach out and 'give more' to those in need.

FEELING LUCKY

While daughters had endured troubled and difficult lives, some nevertheless regard themselves as lucky for life as it now is. They claim that there is much to be positive about and appreciative of in their own lives.

For example, Abbey's bouts of emotional upheaval were offset by the philosophy that there could be someone who is worse off:

I'll say to myself, no matter what happens to me, no matter how tearful or how upset I might get, there's someone out there who's an awful lot worse than I am. I have to be grateful for what I've got.

In recognising the value of her family life, Karen too feels lucky:

We have a great lifestyle, the seven of us. We are very lucky. The children are happy, you know.

The same applies to Helen:

I am very happy in my marriage with my two children and the wider family circle.

Like the others, Kathleen had many unhappy years. However, some of the significant features of her life that she shared in the interview were meeting her husband, her children and success in her education. She happily reports that she feels lucky:

I'm very lucky. I really am. Things have worked out great for me. I'm very, very lucky and I do appreciate that.

What others contribute to their lives is valued and appreciated by daughters. For example, the support gained through siblings seems to strengthen daughters' resolve that they are fortunate:

I suppose maybe in one way myself and [name] are very close, maybe we were lucky that there was two of us and we were able to support each other. I know we are too close, fighting, squabbling and all the rest of it, but I suppose in a strange way we were able to replace that bond with the mother with each other.

Even though Helen endured trauma in her growing-up years, she still values the fact that she has two sisters:

That's the positive out of it. I have a very good relationship with them and that is clearly the positive.

Husbands and partners too are highly regarded for their love, support and understanding. They play a significant role; their input makes a difference. Joanna describes how important it is to know there is someone there who loves her. Occasionally she stops to take stock and realises how lucky she is:

> *Everything is so easy; he's that easy going, he's just a big gentle giant.*

Pauline admits that when she married her husband at the age of seventeen, it took a while to adjust to married life. But she too appreciates that she is blessed with a positive outcome:

> *I'm very lucky in that my husband understands, he really does, because he listens.*

The ability of children to offer help and support is recognised. Children, like Alison's daughter, who offer a listening ear is something that early bereaved daughters in their role as mothers are grateful for:

> *I am very lucky that when I am down [name of daughter] is there and because we have a very open relationship she can come to me and say, 'Mum, just talk about it'. She is very good that way.*

Past, present and future: learn to live with, learn to give in to and move on

As the earlier chapters have shown, the long and arduous journey through loss and grief has been interspersed with coping strategies. However, through their own personal search for meaning, daughters espoused a new outlook. The need to reclaim control and make decisions for the future is recognised as an important task. But reaching a less troubled state can only come about gradually over the years, and, as the testimonies indicate, it is not an easy journey. Nevertheless, somehow, in a life interminably disrupted by the untimely death of their mother, a level of peace and acceptance had been found in more recent years.

While the death and its ramifications had unmistakably influenced her journey, Helen advocates that what has happened in the past was a fate that could not be controlled and that now it is time to let go and move on:

> I can't change what happened in the past; I can't change what happened in my childhood – that was outside of my control. There are so many things that do change how life might have been but I do think it is important to move on. I do think it is important not to dwell on the past and to get to a stage where you can feel you are in control, to the extent that anybody has control of their life.

> To be in control – you can make decisions that will affect your future, you don't have to be totally tied into the past, and it has taken me a long time to realise it. I do firmly feel that I have reached that stage.

From the present day perspective, the journey was reassessed as a process that had many dimensions, as pointed out by Anne. In her particular case there is some consolation in the fact that her mother is 'not completely gone':

> I think, as I say, it's a process, it has to be something that you learn to live with, learn to give in to and move on. I think, be aware. I still talk to her; she will always be a huge presence. People do tell me that I am like her and that I look like her and it's nice to know that – that she's not completely gone.

In Anne's case, the 'presence' and immortality of her mother seems ensured through the inheritance of her personality traits and physical characteristics. When the feedback of others confirms this, it is heartening and welcomed as a reminder that she is 'not completely gone'.

But, it is not surprising that, as daughters reflect on their journey through loss and grief, they find themselves pondering what might have been; Mary:

> I often wondered, had she been there, would things have been different, would things have been easier.

Likewise, Louise grapples with the equally big question:

> *I have no way of knowing how my life would have worked out if my mother had lived, but the actual things that happened to me wouldn't have happened if she had lived.*

Daughters' lives had been irrevocably changed by the experience of the early loss of their mother and the repercussions that ensued. However, their personal philosophies that had evolved across their lifetime indicate that, for some, a new understanding and acceptance had been cultivated.

Examining the current age of participants (in the present study) and their mothers' ages at the time of the death, fifteen had passed the age, two were exactly the same age and nine had not yet reached the age at which the death occurred. Perhaps, whether they were conscious of it or not, daughters had reached the point where they were ready to address the past and look to the future. It was as if they were saying, it's now time to find a balance – let go of that which cannot be changed, make the most of what was good in life, 'move on' and have a say in how the future looks.

Taking part in the study may have signified daughters' readiness to take more control and make choices. In doing so, however, daughters also decided their 'terms of engagement'. For example, when invited to take part in the verification of findings through written feedback or focus groups, many daughters chose the option of writing. Taking part in the focus group would have meant meeting other daughters face to face who had shared the same experience. For some, perhaps emotionally and mentally, this was a step they were not prepared for – a point that was affirmed by maternally bereaved daughters at the presentation (London Conference, July 2005). However, gaining a voice and sharing their experience while remaining anonymous was what most wanted to achieve by taking part in the present study.

The death and loss of a mother in early life is a complex, multi-faceted and multi-layered phenomenon. In summary, daughters' basic need for love, trust and support was significantly challenged by the untimely death and loss of their mother and the repercussions that followed. As a consequence the impact was 'perpetual' and 'pervasive', it is lifelong and ongoing.

In the transition towards a revised way of living, daughters remained steadfast in the desire to retain a 'connection' with their mother. In reflective mode, we discover this to be the case in the words:

I still talk to her; she will always be a huge presence.

ISSUES OF LOSS AND GRIEF: RAISING AWARENESS FOR ALL

As a result of the experiences of the early loss of their mother, daughters in the study had strong views about a number of aspects of early bereavement. To raise awareness, they conveyed messages that they hoped could be passed on to people in the public domain. What they want others to know is that a life-changing event like the loss of a mother is never forgotten and that they continue to carry it with them throughout life.

The issues that daughters distinctly highlighted are summarised as follows:

* Children should be dealt with sensitively around the time of a death. They should not be 'kept away, kept in the dark'. It should be remembered that children grieve too, even though they may be young, that they 'do have thoughts and feelings'. It should be recognised how 'insecure children feel as a result of losing a parent'.

* Children need support in the aftermath of the loss, 'They need help from all quarters – from school, from the family'. Children need to know that there is someone they can talk to. The way in which needs and psychological health are managed following death and loss should be reviewed, as poor care 'only compounds the bereavement'. It was suggested that perhaps family rooms in hospitals could make available guidelines (e.g. posters) regarding how adults could deal with the illness and loss of a child's parent.

* Adults should listen and discuss things with children; they should be aware of 'how important goodbyes are'. The loss should be talked about within the family. In relation to information, it was noted in the written feedback that early bereaved daughters 'place an inordinate amount of importance on any bit of information gleaned, e.g. their mother's favourite flower or beauty product'. It was felt that more should be explained to children prior to, at the time of

the death and afterwards. They should not be kept away from the wake and the funeral. An option should be given to see their mother in the coffin, or at least to see the closed coffin. Children should be offered counselling in the aftermath of the loss to help them to grieve.

❋ When a mother dies, the family is bereaved. It is important in the aftermath of a loss that the family members take care of each other. In the words of one daughter, 'You have to grieve ... but the important thing is to look after the living and who is left, concentrate on them'. Fathers need help and support to cope with the loss although they may not seek it: 'Men need a lot of support to deal with the children and the children need support for the loss of their mother.' Fathers also need help to know what to say to their children about the illness, death and loss of their mother. It was thought that the idea of a 'memory box' that all the family members could look through and discuss in times of need would be helpful.

❋ In the aftermath of the loss, the change in circumstances and conditions within which daughters are reared can result in life being very 'confusing, disorganised and with little structure'. Fathers may form another permanent relationship where a new wife or partner then become stepmother to the children. However, as a result of the loss, children can be vulnerable and at risk, and therefore they should be closely monitored. If support was not available to children within the home, help could be offered in other ways, for example, by psychologists, social workers and teachers. Support is important because the bereavement and the impact of it is 'constantly there'.

❋ Schools could help in a number of ways. First, they could acknowledge the loss, and second, they could consider making changes in the curriculum. That is, bereavement should be included on the school curriculum so that children could have a better understanding of loss and grief. Such education might help children 'prepare' for losses that may occur in the future and help them to become aware of 'the effects' of loss. Schools could also consider carefully the content of lesson plans so that bereaved children are not left feeling uncomfortable in the classroom. Children do not want to be different or singled out as different from their peers in school.

✳ The enormity of the loss of a mother can never be forgotten. 'You come through life with this huge burden on your shoulders' but you cope and get through it. It is important to be sad but it is also important for daughters to know that they can be happy without feeling guilty. Daughters should not underestimate how the loss 'shapes and informs how you interact with the world and that really you do need to find a place to talk about it'. Those daughters who have never talked about the loss of their mother should do so preferably with someone who is 'not related', as those who are related have their own viewpoint. However, daughters should talk only when they are ready. They should seek help in a way that is suitable for them, possibly either through counselling or selecting a teacher to talk to (if they are still in education). Finding a place to talk, through whatever source daughters find helpful, could offer them the opportunity to gain 'insight' into themselves. That is, it might help them to know themselves better and understand why they do things. Daughters should try to find out as much information as they can about what help or services are available. If daughters felt able to speak to other daughters who were maternally bereaved in early life it might help them to hear how others, who had shared the same experience, have fared in life.

SUGGESTED READING

Bowlby, J. (1980), *Attachment and Loss: Loss, Sadness and Depression* (Vol 3), Middlesex: Penguin.

Brown, G.W. and Harris, T. (1978), *Social Origins of Depression*, London: Tavistock.

Erikson, E. H. (1963), *Childhood and Society* (2nd ed.), New York: Norton.

Holland, J. (2001), *Understanding Children's Experiences of Parental Bereavement*, London: Jessica Kingsley.

Nolen-Hoeksema, S. and Larson, J. (1999), *Coping With Loss*, London: Lawerence Erlbaum Associates.

Silverman, P.R. (2000), *Never Too Young To Know. Death in Children's Lives*, London: Oxford University Press.

Worden, W. (1996), *Children and Grief: When a Parent Dies*, New York: The Guilford Press.

ACKNOWLEDGEMENTS

I feel honoured and privileged to be at the helm of a book that gives a 'voice' to early bereaved daughters and is the first of its kind in Ireland. The journey that brought me to this point in my life has been marked with many turning points and opportunities. Without doubt, it is the people I have encountered along the way that have influenced and inspired me, helped me to 'grow', and enabled me to learn and develop, that I have to thank. I owe them all a debt of gratitude for the way in which they have enriched my life. Without them, this volume would never have existed.

- I am deeply indebted to the twenty-six courageous daughters who consented to take part in the interviews and to the five who were able to attend the focus group session that followed later: Mary, Abbey, Patricia, Kathleen, Elaine, Maude, Liz, Elena, Elizabeth, Dara, Helen E, Ann, Joanna, Louise, Lesley, Pauline, Mary B, Karen, Helen, Jennifer, Anne, Theresa, Maureen, Alison, Maggie and Clare. You are the core of this book and without your willingness to share your experiences it would not have been possible to write it.

- I want to pay tribute to Maude who sadly died since the study was completed. With wisdom (and with a little injection of humour at times), Maude openly shared her history and the insights she gained in living with the loss of her mother. I am thankful to her family for allowing their mother's testimony to be included in the book.

- I was very fortunate indeed to have had the assistance, advice and guidance of Donna Doherty, Ruth Kennedy, Linda Longmore and Caitriona Clarke in the preparation and production of this book, and the helpful support of Sinead Scallon, marketing manager. I am especially grateful to Linda who edited most of the chapters. On our first meeting in Dublin I knew that the book was in good hands.

✳ I am forever grateful to those who took the trouble to read and review the book, and for the endorsements they so kindly offered: Dr William Worden, Dr John Holland, Mary Paula Walsh, Dr Ingrid Bacci and Professor Helen Cowie (who wrote the Foreword).

✳ Words cannot express how thankful I am for the help and support of my supervisors of the doctoral study that is the foundation of the book. I would not be where I am without Dr Mary Gallagher (now a principal psychologist with Western Health & Social Services Board) and Dr Rob Millar (University of Ulster). I feel privileged to have had Dr Gallagher's help in developing the PhD and benefited from her massive input in the first three years of the study. My deepest thanks are due to Dr Rob Millar who saw me through the entire five years of the work. His unwavering support and guidance was and is much appreciated.

✳ To my beloved Tracey family: Gerry, John and Joel, thank you for accompanying me on this journey. Even though I spent many long hours with my 'head in the books', it would have been very lonely without love and support around me.

✳ I want to pay homage to my six brothers, Frank, Jack, Brendan, Brian, Desmond and Michael Corey. I deeply appreciate the enduring support that they *and* their wives, Annette, Pat, Phil and the late Monica Corey, have bestowed upon me. They are all very gifted and talented people and they have contributed endlessly to my life. However, when it came to the study and the book, I 'tortured' Brendan, and sometimes Jack, more than the rest. When consulted, Jack offered sound advice and guidance on the style and content of any written piece. Brendan knew about the types of challenges that academic work could pose as he had already achieved a BA from UCD and later a Masters Degree in Social Work from Adelphi University, New York. His input into my life and my work was (and is) precious and invaluable to me. I am truly thankful for his love and support and for that of all my brothers and their families.

❋ To Margaret and Scott Hunter, who are an important part of our lives.

❋ My deepest thanks are due to Carole McKeeman, Nicola Topping and Anna Edwards. You are all busy women and yet you took the time to provide feedback on my work when it was needed. Your input was appreciated and will be remembered.

❋ Thank you Martine (Larfargue-Meenan) for helping me to know and understand myself better through your knowledge, expertise and wisdom as a psychotherapist. The fruits of our incredible five-year journey will stay with me for the rest of my life.

❋ I appreciate the support and encouragement given to me by my colleagues and staff of the School of Psychology at the University of Ulster, especially Dr Mary Jenkins and Karen Kirby. The strength of your support will never be forgotten.

❋ Joanne (of Joanne Mullin Photography), thank you for taking the wonderful pictures of Lia Annette. You are a skilled and talented photographer with a great future.

❋ I am blessed with good friends who listen and care. Even though we don't see each other all the time, I know you are there! I love, respect and admire these amazing women: Kathleen Diamond, Norah Doyle (nee McGlinchey), Christina O'Hagan, Margaret Kearney, Eileen O'Doherty, Pat Hazlett, Pauline Sanz, Sheena Harley, Carole McAdams, Mary McDermott, Claire McGonagle, Esther Loughlin,

Josephine Diamond, Veronica Joyce, Rose White, Dorothy Kenny, Mary Willis, Jacinta Byrne-Doran, Francesca Lundstrom, Vivian Coyle, Monica Barr, Moira McCarthy and Dorothy Millar.

✻ In my education, employment, career and life journey, I have met many supportive and vastly intelligent people who have made a significant contribution, including: Sean O'Kane, Peter Kealey, Bridie Barton, John Murphy, Paul Hammett, Kevin O'Doherty, Michael O'Hanlon, Arthur Barr, the late William Ferguson, Helena McVeigh, Jack Houlahan (author of *A Ghost in Daylight*) and Margaret Coyle. Thank you all.

If you wish to contact the author you can do so by email to: ap.tracey@ulster.ac.uk or in writing to: Dr Anne Tracey, School of Psychology, Room MB018, Magee Campus, University of Ulster, Northland Road, Derry BT48 7JL, Northern Ireland.